Legal Theory Today
Law in its Own Right

Legal Theory Today

General Editor of the Series

Dr John Gardner, Reader in Legal Theory, King's College, London

Forthcoming titles:

Law in its Own Right

Henrik Palmer Olsen
and Stuart Toddington

·H A R T·
PUBLISHING

OXFORD – PORTLAND OREGON
1999

Hart Publishing
Oxford and Portland, Oregon

Published in North America (US and Canada) by
Hart Publishing
c/o International Specialized Book Services
5804 NE Hassalo Street
Portland, Oregon
97213–3644
USA

Distributed in the Netherlands, Belgium and Luxembourg
by
Intersentia, Churchillaan 108
B2900 Schoten
Antwerpen
Belgium

Distributed in Australia and New Zealand by
Federation Press
John St
Leichhardt
NSW 2000

Hart Publishing Ltd is a specialist legal publisher based in
Oxford, England.
To order further copies of this book or to request a list of
other publications please write to:

Hart Publishing Ltd, Salter's Boatyard, Oxford, OX1 4BL
Telephone: +44 (0)1865 245533 or Fax: +44 (0)1865 794882
e-mail: mail@hartpub.co.uk

British Library Cataloguing in Publication Data
Data Available
ISBN 1 84113 034 6 (cloth)
ISBN 1 84113 028 1 (paperback)

Typeset by Hope Services (Abingdon) Ltd.
Printed in Great Britain on acid-free paper
by Biddles Ltd, Guildford and Kings Lynn.

General Editor's Preface

The second half of the twentieth century saw a remarkable explosion of original work in legal theory in the English language, partly a function of broadening intellectual horizons in British and American university law schools, and partly a personal testimony to the ground-breaking contributions of certain individual scholars. Unfortunately it seemed at times that the explosion not only rocked the subject but fragmented it, as different theoretical styles and approaches, with their own intellectual heroes and heroines, sought to establish themselves in the brave new interdisciplinary (and indeed multicultural) world of Anglo-American legal thought. As new sources of intellectual inspiration penetrated the often impatient but always creative legal mind, what should have been argument occasionally turned to enmity, and where there should have been dialogue there was sometimes a hint of disdain.

These were the marks of an academic revolution in its infancy. Now, at the end of the century, it seems that our intellectual insecurities are being replaced with a new and more ecumenical respect for learning. The pioneers of the supposedly rival approaches to legal theory have cascaded their contributions down to an ever widening circle of their students and their students' students, intellectual heirs who have intermingled and intermarried to the point at which, I like to think, ideas are becoming ideas again, as opposed to the totems and taboos of academic tribes. At the same time, and as a corollary, a larger critical mass in the law schools and closer connections with theorists working in other academic milieux have made for a higher general standard of philosophical education and competence, even among those who blushingly like to think of themselves as 'black-letter' lawyers, and even, for that matter, among the most resistant of practice-orientated law students. Together these forces bring us to a point at which the subject is flourishing and, at least in the places I know best, flourishing cordially.

This book series aims to capitalise on this state of affairs. It aims to capture the spirit of open inquiry which comes after a period of exciting but sometimes divisive innovation. The books will therefore serve partly as an encomium for the vast achievements of the last fifty years, but will also push the subject forward, weaving together unexpected and sometimes superficially contrasting strands of thought to yield new and strong argumentative fabrics. Limited to a modest length and published at a modest price in a pocket-sized paperback format, the books are targeted at students and scholars alike, perfect for reading on the bus or in the bath, and, in their pace and tone, associating philosophy as much with ardour as with arduousness. The books take as their mantra the proposition that in legal theory, as in any theoretical field, the best secondary literature—the literature which best documents and assesses what others have already argued—will also turn out to be primary literature in its own right, always framing and defending its own novel positions.

With these aims for the series, it is a particular delight to be launching the series with this fascinating and wide-ranging study by Henrik Palmer Olsen and Stuart Toddington. Their project, fittingly, is to juxtapose and partly harmonise two contrasting thoughts which are very familiar in the history of law and legal science. The first thought is the thought that law exists autonomously, that it can be considered and studied, as the book's title suggests and many lawyers are wont to assume, in its own right. The second thought is the thought of law's surely essential integration into the rest of the Art of Life, its social functions and its allied moral (or claimed-to-be-moral) messages and objectives. The thought, if I may play a little on the title, is that law must have some right to exist, that it cannot by itself make the case for its own existence, that it cannot legitimately lift itself by its own bootstraps. The book reveals, in ways which I found engaging and provocative, the possible dimensions of interplay between these two thoughts and the scope for explaining them not only as compatible, but also as in some ways interdependent. It is an old theme, heightened by modern debates in legal theory, and masterfully synthesised here. It is a fitting entrée to *Legal Theory Today*.

John Gardner
King's College London
15 July 1999

Acknowledgements

Writing for this new series has not only been a privilege and a rare opportunity that we were very proud to accept, but it has also been immensely rewarding and enjoyable to have had the chance to work with John Gardner and Richard Hart. The imaginative advice and encouragement we received from John Gardner has made this a much better book than it could ever have been without him. Similarly, we could not have hoped for more enthusiastic and expert attention than that which we received from the team at Hart Publishing.

We would like to thank The Institute of Legal Science B at the University of Copenhagen, and The Department of Legal Studies at the University of Central Lancashire for their generous and enthusiastic support throughout the project. Henning Koch, Peter Blume and Chris Bovis are particularly deserving in this regard. In addition we would like to acknowledge the invaluable help of S.B (*Banu*) Murtuja and Philip Bielby for their comments and suggestions on early drafts of the manuscript. Last, but certainly not least, we want to say a special 'thank you' to the unique and remarkable Christiane Olsen.

HPO and ST
August 1999

Contents

1

The State of Legal Theory Today

Herbert Hart, in introducing *The Concept of Law*, speaks of the unique miseries of legal scholars in relation to the question 'What is Law?'. No vast literature, he observes, is to be found dedicated to the questions, 'What is Chemistry?' or 'What is Medicine?'. This is not entirely true; but Hart's laconic reference does highlight a curious disparity in relation to what is, on the face of it, a faintly ridiculous inquiry.

There are, however, more direct and less embarrassing ways of initiating a debate into what, plainly, is more than a request to be instructed in the usage of a simple word. One is to try the honest option and ask what all the fuss is about. Orthodoxly, the fuss about the concept of law has been characterised in terms of, if not distinct, then certainly longstanding divisions over the proposition that there either is, or is not, a 'necessary' or conceptual connection between law and morality. There are, no doubt, many dimensions to this particular aspect of jurisprudential inquiry, but in our view, and what might serve as the central contention of this book, there is little point to the law and morality dispute unless the role of moral judgement in the philosophical determination of the concept of law is acknowledged to relate directly to the issue of the *obligation to obey*. Organisational or procedural descriptions and classifications of 'legal' systems as opposed to 'customary' or 'pre-legal' systems, although informative and useful in other ways, fail to do this.[1] Thus, on

---

[1] For example, Unger's ideal types or 'forms' of law, and Hart's distinction between 'primary' and 'secondary' rules are of immense significance to our sociological understanding of the development of normative organisation in society, but although they can tell us much about the evolution and configuration of power and interests, we maintain that the problem of obligation resists all

the basis of acknowledging that law, ultimately, is coercive, and given that we can appreciate the irony of being 'obliged' to do something at the point of a gun, we might begin by way of the question, 'What is the distinction, if any, between legal obligation and moral obligation?'

This approach does not relieve us of the task of attempting to determine a defensible and non-arbitrary concept of law; nor, as a matter of logical priority, of explicating the methodology of concept formation appropriate to the task. But these fundamental matters are at least given some orientation if we are introduced to them by way of responding to a determinate and engaging question. Our question presupposes but does not, of course, prove that there are, in fact, any genuine obligations; but it at once concentrates the mind to consider the utility of a concept of law which does not offer a candid discussion of obligation in general and a satisfactory account of the above distinction in particular.

The Obligation to Obey

Furthermore, if the distinction between legal and moral obligation is, at least preliminarily, to be the object of genuine philosophical inquiry, let us not begin with the presumptuous assertion (which at best demands careful scrutiny and an immense amount of qualification) that there might be 'immoral', yet 'legally valid' rules, but rather let us note less ambitiously that the general acknowledgement of some form of a relationship between law and morality can hardly be avoided by anyone prepared to recognise the broad intelligibilty of the two terms. This, of course, does not preclude the possibility of disagreement over the precise character of the relationship in question. This is to be expected when we note that it is often unclear, for example, whether the participants in the debate understand the issue as (a), a descriptive matter concerning the actual employ-

'descriptive' accounts of law. See Unger, R.M., *Law in Modern Society* (Free Press, New York, 1976) chap. 2; Hart, H.L.A., *The Concept of Law* (Clarendon, Oxford, 1961); also see Chap. 2 *infra*.

ment of moral reasoning in the history, practices and decision-making of personnel operating in a set of formal institutions, or whether (b), the relationship between law and morality is to be understood as expressing a prescriptive and critical ideal 'immanent' in the 'essential' concept of law. The former approach, (a), if unadulterated, lies closer to lexicographical and biographical concerns and, logically speaking, is largely inadequate to the type of analysis suggested by the question. The latter, (b), expresses an epistemological intent which, in terms of the essential understanding of legal concepts such as validity and obligation, must inevitably encompass the wider issue of legitimacy in society and thus shares common ground with the methodological problems of political philosophy and the social sciences. By examining some of the foundational issues raised in these latter disciplines we think that we can more usefully re-locate and re-present many of the apparent disagreements over the nature of 'the necessary connection' between law and morality.

Our view is that law should be understood—perhaps we should say reconstructed *a priori* for theoretical purposes—as arising from the implications of a reliance on practical reason to resolve regulatory and co-ordinatory problems in a social context. That is, law can be seen as the practically reasonable attempt to institutionalise and uphold in a society certain practical norms, which, because of the special authority which has arisen in the institutions and offices responsible for the positing, application and enforcement of those norms, are seen to possess a legitimate priority—an *exclusionary* validity—as against other norms in that society. This view is hardly unorthodox. It employs the familiar and circular dependence of the notion of legality on the idea of *legitimacy* as it relates to the *authority* of an institutional system to posit and enforce valid norms, and, hence, alludes to a reciprocally justified obligation to obey.[2] This obligation, because of the implicit appeals to, or assumptions of,

---

[2] This is a widely accepted notion of authority. Raz appears to dispute it, however. *Cf.* e.g., Kant, Immanuel, *The Metaphysics of Morals* (Mary Gregor (trans., ed.) Cambridge University Press, Cambridge, 1996) at 25, 26; and Raz, Joseph, *The Authority of Law* (Clarendon Press, Oxford, 1978), chap. 1.

legitimacy and validity, is thus presented as qualitatively different from brute dominion, coercion and submission in terms of arbitrary commands backed by threats of violence. This is markedly obvious if we reflect upon the expectation that rule-makers and rule-enforcers are themselves subject to the rules. These are undoubtedly the conceptual ingredients of a coherent and comprehensive theoretical account of law, but the potentially tautologous nature of this circle, we argue, can be broken only by grounding one or another of the appeals to legitimacy (or normative validity) in a general argument which demonstrates the practical rationality of the initial acceptance of effective social incorporation leading to institutionalised obligations.

The issue of obligation, as we have already pointed out, is our organising concept. The task, then, can be seen as the problem of developing a concept of law from an account of a form of obligation which lies problematically between, on the one hand, pure (subjective) morality and, on the other, naked physical coercion. This is a subtle undertaking, in that there exists an important form of obligation lying between these two poles: that of the complex network of traditional or customary allegiances, social pressures and expectations.[3] This much is brilliantly, if inconclusively, discussed by Herbert Hart in *The Concept of Law*, and impressively, but problematically, analysed by Joseph Raz in his *The Authority of Law*.[4] Two preliminary observations may be noted in relation to these influential texts.

The first, in Hart, is that although it is a useful classificatory exercise to show that legal obligation differs from subjective and voluntaristic forms of obligation, customary obligation and obligation under naked threat, the mere process of differentiation (combined, as we explain below, with general allusions to social order or 'functional necessity') does not provide a justificatory basis for that which is, admittedly, so clearly differentiated.

---

[3] See, for example, Poggi, Gianfranco, *The Development of the Modern State: A Sociological Introduction* (Hutchinson, London, 1978) See also Unger, Roberto M., *Law in Modern Society* (n. 1 *supra*), chap. 2.

[4] Cf. Hart, H.L.A., *The Concept of Law* (n. 1 *supra*) and Raz, J., *The Authority of Law* (n. 2 *supra*), chaps. 1 and 8.

Rather, far from making a case for the acceptance of a non-moral concept of obligation, Hart, seems to show only that a moral conception of obligation is the sole remaining coherent option.[5]

Secondly, this much seems to be precisely the view to which Raz is resigned in his exceptionally acute analysis of the correlative relations which obtain between, on the one hand, authority and, on the other, practically rational compliance. It is extremely illuminating to note that he shows clearly that the concept of authority consistent with a *non-moral* concept of law implies that we must abandon the idea that there is, strictly speaking, a general obligation to obey law. This argument, positivistically speaking, is perfectly sound. But given the absolutely pivotal role of the concept of obligation in the *differentiation* of law as a form of regulation distinct from voluntarism, custom and sheer threat, we take Raz's argument, rather, as a powerful *reductio ad absurdum* of the general claims of legal positivism.

A Wider Theoretical Context

The problems raised above are not, we think, intractable. However, they cannot be resolved within a discrete discipline ('law') assumed to have a privileged insight, but, rather, must be progressively clarified through an examination of the moral epistemology which is usually implicit, if not entirely repressed, in modern social theory and political philosophy. However, such is the power of the *idea* of legality and so vivid is the illusion of its 'facticity', that it appears to retain sufficient normative and moral autonomy to elude the scrutiny of critique and the rigours of the theory of political obligation. How does this come about?

We might begin to explain it first in terms of what we perceive to be a methodological sleight of hand common to the fundamental assumptions of both structuralist sociology and classical political philosophy. In particular, and respectively, we have in

[5] See especially Hart n. 4 *supra*, 79–86 and also 163–80.

mind the notion of society as a self-regulating, normative system or structure;[6] and the idea of the transition from a 'state of nature' to civil society by way of a 'social contract'.[7] Whilst these ideas may be helpful in terms of a general description of the functional evolution of forms of legal order, influential examples of social theory and political philosophy have exhibited the tendency to prioritise uncritically the value of the normative stability of the *status quo*. This leads to a neglect of (possibly valid and important) alternative perspectives in the complexity and plurality of social and economic interests. We can take the opportunity to highlight the pivotal issues here by examining the way in which the contribution of legal positivism can be seen as a revealing attempt to integrate social and political theory in responding to the problem of the apparent indeterminacy of the claims of political morality which characterise conditions of interest plurality.

The background concern of legal positivism arises from the idea, axiomatic in the social and anthropological sciences, that individuals as well as sub-groups of society must acknowledge the need for a stable and predictable stock of common norms in response to the regulatory and co-ordinatory problems facing any significantly complex social group. In order for such a system to persist, it is necessary that the society as a whole, as well

---

[6] Durkheim is of seminal importance here but Giddens notes that:

'Durkheim's discussion of functional and causal explanation in sociology . . . has been remarkably influential, although it is quite cursory. "Function", he argued, must be clearly distinguished from "intention" or "purpose" . . . the function of . . . activity is to enhance social unity. The function of a social item refers, in Durkheim's phrase, to its correspondence with "the general needs of the social organism" ' (Giddens, A., *Durkheim* (Fontana, London, 1978), 390).

See also n. 8 *infra*, and Chap. 3 *infra*.

[7] For an overview see e.g., Minogue, K., 'Thomas Hobbes and the Philosophy of Absolutism' in Thompson, D., *Political Ideas* (Penguin, London, 1966), chap. 4; Cole, G.D.H., 'Introduction to Rousseau, J.J.', *The Social Contract and Discourses* (Dent, Everyman's Library, 1983), pp. xi–xlv; Barker, Sir E., *Social Contract: Essays by Locke, Hume, Rousseau* (Oxford University Press, London, 1971), Introduction, vii–xliv; also Kant (n. 2 *supra*), p. xiv ff.

as sub-groups and individuals, acknowledge the need for some of the members of society to perform the tasks of articulating or selecting and enforcing those norms that should be applied in society. This model has been a point of departure for all of our most influential social, political and jurisprudential writers from Hobbes to Durkheim and beyond. It is, in fact, a conceptually unavoidable result of reflecting on the nature of a social group, and thus it is rightly regarded as fundamental. However, it is a long way from providing a theory of legal, political or moral obligation. Let us reflect for a moment on two forms of its use and abuse in wider theory.

First, sociologically, it has formed the basis of the structuralist or 'systems theory' approach. In Durkheim and Marx, no less than in more recent attempts by Luhmann[8] to present legality as an indispensable 'system-function', we see the idea of society as a functional organism imbued with a inherent tendency to integral preservation—stability, order, equilibrium. The biological origins of this metaphor are well known, and there can be no doubt that once normative institutions or sub-systems are presented as analogues of biological sub-systems, explanations in terms of their interrelations in providing overall system stability seem perfectly plausible. There are, however, two serious problems with this approach.

In a large body of influential (and not necessarily conservative) social theory, as Merton rightly points out, the sociologically indispensable idea of a social *structure* implies the notion of *function* in its component institutional parts.[9] The idea of the necessity of order or equilibrium of the social system, then, seems to be enough to explain or account for the existence of certain normative institutions. It is a short step to argue from an account of the rationale of their existence *vis-à-vis* 'the system' to the assumption of the rationality of individual compliance with their normative content. This means that the idea of functional necessity ultimately becomes an issue of morality. But the

[8] See, e.g., Luhman, N., 'Operational Closure and Structural Coupling: The Differentiation of the Legal System' (1992) 13 *Cardozo L. Review* 1419.

[9] See our discusion in Chap. 3 *infra*.

issue of obligation—that is, the issue of the rational justification of demands for compliance with norms—or the moral worth of institutions *per se* is an issue which positivist sociology might easily side-step; thus the matter can be left at that. Our point— particularly in Chapter 3—will be that this unsatisfactory ellipsis is equally applicable to jurists (e.g. Llewellyn, Hart) who present apparently plausible *descriptive* conceptions of the legal enterprise heavily supplemented by allusions to the idea of obligation inherent in the background structure of social necessity.

Secondly, the axiom of social incorporation leading to an institutionalised system of obligations—i.e. the idea of the state—has its classical expression in social contract theory. Hobbes famously begins from a problematic state of nature where danger and instability reign. In Hobbes, the sheer savagery and perennial conflict of the state of nature is presented as an almost self-evidently valid *prudential* reason for each and every individual to surrender their 'natural freedom' and recognise the authority of a sovereign law-giver. The genius of Hobbes lies in the fact that he goes a long way to establishing an impressive model of the authority of law and state from an apparently moral vacuum. The price to be paid for this achievement *ex nihilo* is the acceptance of the absolute power and unquestionable discretion of the sovereign. This is the illiberal consequence of the *quid pro quo* of obedience for protection. Locke, however, offers a more attractive version of the contract starting from the existence in the state of nature of God-given rights to property and personal safety, as well as the right to punish. The contract merely formalises these natural rights. In this way Locke appears to refute the thesis of absolutism by presenting these fundamental rights as the obvious limits to the legitimate exercise of power within the state. But Hobbes was so clearly one step ahead of this modification. He advocated absolutism as a response to the problem of *interpretation of laws* which inevitably arises in any model of the contract—natural rights or no natural rights.[10] Let us consider it briefly.

---

[10] Hobbes, T., *Leviathan* (C.B. McPherson (ed.), London, Pelican, 1968), Part II, chap. 26, 322. See also Chap. 5 *infra*.

In most modern, democratic polities the rules about who has the competence to do what in relation to the common stock of norms, are ostensibly set out explicitly in a written constitution. Two major problems now arise. The first is, precisely what do the appointed authorities have authority to do? This question can be subdivided into (a) what is the practical *rationale* of establishing this form of societal incorporation *ab initio*? and (b) what should be the contents and limits of a constitutional power thenceforth? Both of these sub-issues arise very clearly in the contemporary jurisprudential debate and, we will argue, are identical to the concerns proceeding from the premisses of classical social contract theory. It is here, in the intersection between political philosophy and constitutional law, that we will look for answers to the jurisprudential problem of the conditions and limits of legal validity.

The second problem consists in this: once the institutionalisation of a common stock of norms has come about, there arises the task of interpreting and applying these norms to specific and concrete situations. This is a task which involves much more than identifying something like a Hartian 'rule of recognition' which might, initially, lead us to the raw material of the normative stock; that is, the bluntly posited yet uninterpreted, uncontextualised statement of norms. It is here, we think, that the legal positivist's justifiable concern with the need for, and value of, certainty and predictability in the normative life of a society seems to undermine itself. We will argue that the coherence of the broadly positivist case against moral reasoning in law runs into difficulty on two fronts. First, at the point where the logical procedures, methods or habits of interpretation and application of the normative raw material become, from the point of view of those subject to them, *opaque*; that is, when the prudential and co-ordinatory rationale of norm interpretation and application becomes—theoretically or actually—unfathomable or unpredictable. Transparency in this regard, we will argue, is crucially implicit in the *raison d'être* of establishing a common 'positive' stock of norms. Mere finality of decision-making or 'legal certainty' divorced from public reasoning rooted in the social purpose of authoritative incorporation contradicts and defeats the theoretical bases of a positivist account of legal validity. Secondly, and equally troubling, a legal positivistic understanding of law's 'autonomy' from morality becomes incoherent when the theoretical account of the processes of interpretation and application acknowledges that these processes are, or may legitimately be, conditioned and informed by interests and values drawn from the *initially problematic* stock of conflicting political moralities.

'Autonomy' and 'Artificiality'

Ironically, this very problem arises dramatically in much that has been recently and enthusiastically articulated in favour of a legal positivist view of the idea that law is 'autonomous' from morality. We are aided here by Gerald Postema's important analysis of the normative-logical anatomy of the general assumptions of the thesis of the 'autonomy' of law which appear to underpin a plethora of attempts to present the legitimacy of law and legal obligations in non-moral terms.[11] By looking at what is involved in the attempt to separate law from morality *via* some version of what Postema refers to as the Autonomy Thesis, we think that we can make a clear and compelling case for the integration of law and morality in the general scheme of practical reason.

This is an argument which requires careful articulation in that one must acknowledge the common-sensical rightness inherent in legal positivism's attempt to conceive of law as a form of legitimate normativity, which can be separated (is autonomous) from the *direct* application of (for the sake of argument, possibly objective and demonstrable) moral principles. Law, according to the theory of legal positivism, consists of those norms which are produced by the institutional arrangements which are alleged to arise as a functional or

[11] See Postema, G., 'Law's Autonomy and Public Practical Reason' in George, R.P. (ed.), *The Autonomy of Law: Essays on Legal Positivism* (Clarendon, Oxford, 1996), 79–119.

political response to problematic conditions of complexity. But there are limits to how far this can get us in achieving a full understanding of the legal enterprise. For once doubt can be raised either in relation to the correct understanding of the nature of the these conditions giving rise to the need for the social contract (i.e. the account of the practical reasoning leading to the institutional prioritisation of a set of authoritative norms), or in relation to the logic of in corporation and its bearing on the correct or permissible interpretation of one of the norms posited by the legal authorities, we see that swift recourse to the idea of 'the autonomy' of law raises more questions than it can answer. That is, we must start to ask moral questions—and come up with moral answers—to issues concerning the nature, purpose and scope of the very idea of an institutionalised form of 'autonomous' normativity.

But assuming that this moral insight might be achieved, we are not suggesting that this settles or clarifies at a stroke the issue of the nature of the relationship between the legal and the moral. For we must accept that what distinguishes legal reasoning from moral reasoning *simpliciter* is that legal reasoning is concerned not only with the question of justification, but with the question of *application and enforcement* of practical norms under complex and imperfect circumstances. It is these imperfect circumstances, and the functional requirements of enforceable, authoritative determinations of judgements of value that give rise to the obvious differences in approaches to reasoning which characterise law in its *practical* application as opposed to morality understood *theoretically*. But this should not lead us hastily to assume that legality and morality are therefore *qualitatively* distinct. Legal positivism has rightly emphasised the need for an autonomous sphere of practical reason established specifically to respond to the co-ordinatory and regulatory problems of moral indeterminacy and societal complexity. There is a clear pragmatic requirement for an authoritative cut-off point for moral argument, and that the setting up of social institutions to meet this need will entail the formation of an 'artificial' (as opposed to 'natural') discourse. This distinction is hardly novel. Coke in his famous decision from 1607, says[12]:

> true it was that god had endowed His Majesty with excellent science, and great endowments of nature; but His Majesty was not learned in the laws of his realm of England, and causes which concern the life, or inheritance, or goods, or fortunes of his subjects, are not to be decided by natural reason, but by the artificial reason and judgment of law, which law is an act which requires long study and experience, before that a man can attain to the cognizance of it . . .

It is important to acknowledge that there is such an 'artificial' realm of practical reason inhabited by law, but let us not concede that this realm is entirely self-supporting or self-generating. This becomes clear when one attempts to conceptualise the *rationale* behind the original formation of such an 'artificial' (autonomous) realm. Let us not forget that, at some point, the argument for a legitimate, authoritative and enforceable stock of autonomous norms, as Gerald Postema makes clear, has (theoretically) to appear as a practically reasonable first step from all perspectives of interest, and, thenceforth, to continue to appear reasonable. Given this rather onerous set of conditions, against the value-neutral or broadly positivist view, we might say, Hobbes notwithstanding, that a merely prudential or 'functionally' pragmatic account of the legal enterprise has an enormous amount of justificatory work to perform with very scant conceptual resources.

Naturalism and Positivism

These reflections may go some way to lending rational plausibility to the core of a natural law or legal idealist perspective. This approach to understanding law is not accurately represented as the assertion that all rules posited as 'laws', or all rules which happen to have had this nomenclature ascribed to them, are, *ipso facto*, morally just. Rather, a coherent legal idealism suggests that a rational understanding of the conception of the legal enterprise leads us to the conclusion that rules posited as laws

---

[12] *Prohibitions Del Roy—Case of Prohibitions* (1607) 12 Co. Rep. 63.

ought to meet certain demands of morality *if* they are to achieve validity as laws.[13] Legal validity, in this sense, and when ascribed to a rule or a system of rules, implies a moral justification to promulgate and enforce, and consequently implies the existence of an obligation to obey. Moral rationality, legal validity and legal obligation are, therefore, held to be conceptually inseparable. Natural law or legal idealism is thus the thesis that, philosophically speaking, a valid legal order ought to be understood as being constituted by the moral legitimacy of its procedural and substantive norms. This presupposes the possibility of rational access to a core of morality which is objective in the sense that rational persons may not only identify it, but acknowledge the bindingness of its general prescriptions. But this does not mean that the natural lawyer must hold that all interpretations and applications of these principles in, and to, complex circumstances are infallible, uncontentious or, in practice, entirely and uniquely determinate.[14]

Conversely, the legal positivist who argues for a functionalist[15] concept of law is not necessarily morally insensitive. Rather, the concern of the positivist is to overcome what he or she sees as the real danger to modern complex societies, namely the arbitrariness of power which poses a potential danger to the very idea of a legal order. Morality, so the argument goes, if not actually facilitative of abuse, is unable, in and of itself, to produce solutions to many of the co-ordinatory problems of modern society. If one allows subjective moral considerations to overrule positive enacted laws, then social life suffers damage infinitely worse than what might result from the acceptance of the 'validity', and hence the enforcement, of some allegedly 'immoral' rules.[16]

---

[13] A detailed explanation is to be found in Beyleveld, Deryck, and Brownsword, Roger, *Law as a Moral Judgment* (Sweet and Maxwell, London, 1986), 43–61.

[14] See *ibid.*, 374 ff.; also our discussion in Chap. 6 *infra*.

[15] See Chap. 3 *infra* for a full discussion of functionalist tendencies in jurisprudence.

[16] See our discussion of Radbruch in Chap. 2 *infra*; also of Ingeborg Maus's views in Chap. 4 *infra.*, and in 'Idealism for Pragmatists', *Archiv für Recht und Sozialphilosophie* 4/99.

Let us say straight away that acknowledging the good sense of this latter position, that is, conceding that morality in complex contexts might be 'indeterminate', is not equivalent to admitting that morality is thus unstable and arbitrary. Rather, we should acknowledge that moral rationality might admit of a plurality of *simultaneously reasonable solutions* to a particular problem. This should not be seen as an argument *against* moral objectivism or as an argument *for* the need to construct a value-neutral concept of law. This wish for perfectionism in the sense that moral reason must be expected to deliver 'the one right answer' is a misunderstanding of the issue and, we, think, a misunderstanding of what Ronald Dworkin has in mind when employing this phrase in defence of 'the best interpretation' in a morally integral concept of law.[17] Morality does not require perfection, nor does it even require success. *'Ought'* undeniably implies *'can'*; and thus we cannot reasonably ask for more than a good faith attempt to imbue legal reasoning with moral rationality.[18] It is entirely unhelpful, therefore, to begin the study of jurisprudence by suggesting that natural law or legal idealism is in some sense the antithesis of legal positivism. Instead we find it much more productive to work on the assumption that the worries which drive some to argue strongly for legal positivism are in fact shared by those who argue strongly for natural law, and *vice versa*. Looking at the jurisprudential dispute in this way, the schism arising from the issue of the relationship between law and morals comes more to look like a matter of a difference in emphasis. We think that more progress can be made if we begin our analysis by directing our attention to the plausible case for a conception of law in terms of an acknowledgement of the

[17] See Dworkin, R., *Law's Empire* (Fontana Press, London, 1986), chap. 6. See also our discussion in Chap. 6 *infra*.

[18] See Radbruch on this idea in Section 2, 'Legal Philosophy as the Evaluating View of Law 2' especially at 57f. in the translation by Wilk, K., *The Legal Philosophies of Lask, Radbruch, and Dabin* (Harvard University Press, Cambridge, Mass., 1950). We discuss this in more detail in Chap. 2 *infra*; Beyleveld, and Brownsword address this issue in *Law as a Moral Judgment* (n. 13 *supra*), 45.

interplay between the requirements of practical functionality and the intuitively moral quest for a form of legitimacy, and reflect upon why, *prima facie*, this appears to militate against a moral conception of law and legal obligation. But before attempting to unravel this issue in Chapter 2, it will be useful to examine a few contributory issues which may find some resonance with the concerns of other readers familiar with the field of inquiry. We have selected five points upon which we hope to elaborate in more detail as the chapters of the book unfold. For the moment we will introduce them in a way which hints at their interrelations and which offers some guidance to the structure of our overall argument.

Methodological and Substantive Ambiguities

Perhaps the first point to be made concerns the debilitating ambiguity of argument inherent in jurisprudential discourse. Traditionally, the opposition between, on the one hand, legal positivism and, on the other, natural law theory or legal idealism is cited; but the disparate nature of the theories held to belong to one camp or the other makes it almost impossible to identify the disputants. Stephen Perry, writing recently about Wil Waluchov's attempt to argue for a form of 'inclusive' legal positivism, says[19]:

> It is not easy to come up with a characterization of legal positivism that is not vacuous and yet at the same time is sufficiently general to capture the myriad theories of law to which, over the years, the positivist label has been attached.

This is perfectly true. In fact, as we will presently note, it is probably true that the practical-theoretical difference not only among versions of legal positivism, but between certain accounts of positivism and certain natural law perspectives, is probably unidentifiable. But this merely reinforces what we find to be

[19] Perry, S.R., 'The Varieties of Legal Positivism' (1996) ix *Canadian Journal of Law and Jurisprudence* 361.

unsatisfactory: ambiguity of argument or subject matter *per se* is no virtue.

A not uncommon characterisation of legal positivism, however, resides in the claim that the connection between law and morality is 'contingent' as opposed 'necessary'. But hope of enlightenment through this proposition is fleeting and illusory. For even if the affirmation (or the denial) of this contingent connection was to be made clear, and even if we might settle on what was intended by 'contingent' as opposed to 'necessary' in this regard, we must note that the debate within positivism is often not substantively concerned with law *as an object of investigation*, but, rather, displays a methodological preoccupation with 'law' *as a discipline* conceived sometimes as sociological description, sometimes as sociological critique. Let us pursue this point for a moment. Perry's comparatively recent and extremely readable review of Waluchow offers us a continuing and convenient example of the nature of the debate. He says[20]:

> Methodological positivists maintain that legal theory is a purely descriptive, non-normative enterprise that sets out, in the manner of ordinary science, to tell us what one particular corner of the world we inhabit is like. Substantive positivists defend one version or another of the thesis, identified by Waluchow as the core of legal positivism, that there are no necessary connections between law and morality. These are, logically, distinct claims. There is nothing obviously inconsistent or incoherent in a methodological positivist supporting the natural law view that there is, in the world as we find it, a necessary connection *of some kind* [our emphasis] between law and morality . . .
>
> There is also nothing obviously inconsistent or incoherent about a theorist adopting a non-positivist jurisprudential methodology, presumably on the grounds that it is impossible to formulate a normatively neutral theory of law, in order to defend the substantive positivist thesis that there are no necessary connections between law and morality.

[20] Perry, S.R., 'The Varieties of Legal Positivism' (1996) ix *Canadian Journal of Law and Jurisprudence* 361.

Obvious or not, only obfuscation can, in our view, save these configurations from inconsistencies, and in Chapter 3 we will explore the matter of methodology in the social sciences more fully. But for the moment let us note that *essentially* this debate has nothing to do with natural law or legal positivism. Rather, it raises a particular aspect of the general question as to whether it is either possible or desirable that social science should model itself on the allegedly descriptive and 'value free' methods of the natural sciences. This problem, ultimately, rests upon whether the 'practical' or 'meaningful' nature of social phenomena, as opposed to 'law-governed' natural phenomena, must be modelled 'ideal-typically' in accordance with some *essential* conception of purposive rationality or, alternatively, from some 'internal' or 'participatory' point of view. This raises the question not so much of objectivity in *description*, but whether the cognitive orientation of social science seeks to know what law is *essentially*, or seeks to record and report what some participants in the enterprise variously and *arbitrarily* conceive it to be. This is a question about what social science is, not what law is; and this methodological question remains identical whether we are interested in the theoretical appropriation of law, or the family or gender or religion.[21] And if it is at this methodological point that the issue of the conceptual intrusion of value-judgement or 'morality' occurs, we may as well ask whether or not there is a necessary connection between *any* institutional phenomenon and morality. If there can be no value-free sociology, then the answer must be affirmative. Does this, however, automatically settle the issue in favour of natural law or legal idealism as against legal positivism? Perhaps not. There are at least three reasons for the persistence of disagreement.

First, methodological ambiguity takes an exponentially more confused turn when we note that between the poles of normative and non-normative methodologies there appears to be a

---

[21] On this important Weberian point, see Toddington, S., *Rationality, Social Action and Moral Judgment* (Edinburgh University Press, Edinburgh, 1993), chap. 2. See also Chap. 3 *infra.*

case for defending a soggy patch of middle ground. Again, Perry is of great help to us in outlining an example of the approach. In explaining Waluchow's approach to the critique of Dworkin, he observes that[22]:

> Waluchow . . . concedes that a descriptive explanatory theory 'can be based upon and even guided by non-moral, evaluative considerations' such as simplicity, the principle of charity and coherence . . .. Evaluative judgments, possibly moral in nature, concerning what is and is not significant may also guide the theorist in picking out aspects of social practice as appropriate ones on which to centre his descriptive-explanatory theories. Given these concessions, Waluchow can perhaps be described as a moderate methodological positivist.

This should not be seen as some matter specific to Stephen Perry or Wil Waluchow—there are many examples of this debate. The point we wish to make *vis-à-vis* ambiguity is that this type of methodological approach could eventually culminate in the less than inspirational thesis that there is a *moderate* connection *in some sense* between law and morality. Unremarkable in itself, this view gives rise to vacillation concerning the problem of legal validity which, we will argue, undermines and devalues a significant proportion of contemporary debate. The following, second reason, provides a particularly important example of this.

This concerns the ambiguity which persists in idealist and positivist conceptions of law which permits equivocation on the term 'morality' such that methodological *and* substantive natural lawyers (like John Finnis), can agree with methodological and substantive *positivists* (such as Neil MacCormick), to the effect that there is *both* a necessary connection between law and morality, and that yet there are immoral yet 'legally valid' rules.[23] This, however, in our view, and as we shall explain in Chapter

---

[22] Perry (n. 20 *supra*), 364.

[23] This is what Lucy refers to as the curious *'entente cordiale'* between naturalism and positivism: see Lucy, William, 'Natural Law Now' (1992) 56 *Modern Law Review* 745–60.

2, is merely a restatement of the problem in the equally ambiguous terms of 'legal validity'.

The third reason, not unrelated to those immediately noted, concerns what we have already noted to be an idea of central importance: the notion of the *autonomy* (from morality) of law. Essentially, following Gerald Postema, the Autonomy Thesis[24] states that although law arises historically (and possibly methodologically) from moral concerns, it is the very nature of moral conflict which behoves us to remove legal reasoning from this sphere of intractable striving. So, where, on the basis of accepting the value-laden nature of methodological concept formation, this thesis is subsequently employed as the basis of an attempt to theorise and justify a non-moral conception of *legal obligation*, we are then presented with a persuasive and unambiguous version of legal positivism. Unambiguous first, because it acknowledges the independence of the methodological problem, and secondly, because it takes the issue of the relationship between law and morality to relate directly to the problem of whether legal obligation is a form of moral obligation. Ironically, however, it seems that the nearest we get to this formulation is presented as a version of 'natural law'.[25]

Rather than attempt to reformulate legal positivism or its antitheses to the satisfaction of those who might wish to celebrate the nuances, and in the absence of convenient self-ascription, our understanding of the issue is structured in terms of *purely hypothetical* polar extremes. That is, at one pole let us imagine a theoretical position which is entirely antithetical to the intrusion of moral reasoning in legal reasoning; at the other, and conversely, the thesis that legal reasoning cannot genuinely exist and manifest itself as valid law unless it essentially and consistently incorporates moral reasoning. One pole is reasonably designated as a 'legal positivist' position, the other as a 'natural law' or 'legal idealist' position. But these distinctions are merely

[24] See Postema (n. 11 s*upra*).

[25] See generally Finnis, J., *Natural Law and Natural Rights* (Clarendon Press, Oxford, 1980); but especially, Finnis, J., 'The Truth in Legal Positivism' in George (n. 11 *supra*), 195–215.

convenient and preliminary forms of nomenclature. In Chapter 2 we want to show how attempts to articulate more or less 'positivistic' arguments implicitly make concessions to their antitheses. We do this with a view to clarifying, in subsequent analysis (particularly in Chapters 5 and 6), how the formation of legal concepts might avoid these contradictions.

The Characterisation of Morality

Our second point concerns the presupposition, implicit in much influential discourse concerning the relationship between law and morality, that there initially and unproblematically exists a basic and coherent opposition or separation between law and morality. Whilst we do not wish to suggest that law and morality are identical, we are disturbed by the tendency to characterise morality either as private, subjective and voluntaristic, or perhaps as some form of popular, but essentially optional, system of *mores* and preferences.[26] This begs the question in respect of the problem of the nature of the connection between law and morals in that law is often automatically—and not incorrectly—presented as objective, factual, codified and non-optional. The result of uncritically assuming the mutual exclusivity of this opposition, however, inevitably leads us to infer that whatever the connection between law and morals, it must, perforce, be a contingent one.

More technically, in, for example, Habermas, Maus and a host of 'anti-rationalist', 'post-Cartesian' and 'communitarian' texts, this essentially lay understanding is reproduced in the form of a dichotomous and irreconcilable opposition between 'monological' and 'dialogical' reason.[27] The former, seen as an

[26] This is a lay tendency but is to be found, e.g. in Hart. See *The Concept of Law* (n. 2 *supra*), 163–6.

[27] See e.g. Habermas, J., *Between Facts and Norms* (Polity Press, Cambridge, 1996), 224; Maus, Ingeborg, 'The Differentiation Between Law and Morality as a Limitation of Law' in: Aarnio, A., and Tuori, K. (eds.), *Law, Morality and Discursive Rationality* (Publications of the Departments of Public Law, University of Helsinki, Helsinki, 1988), 143. For a critique see Toddington (n. 21 *supra*), 154–6.

individualistic, objectivating and rationalistic form of reason is alleged to characterise moral thinking and is perjoratively contrasted with the participatory, communicative, consensualist—in short, collective and democratic—associations of the latter. In respect of the relationship between law and morality, the argument seems to be that morality runs with individualism, unaccountability and unpopular impositions of authority, and that law (and society) is democratically better off without it. This claim we examine in some detail in Chapter 4.

Against these unhelpful and, we will argue, fallacious oppositions, we want to argue that whilst it is important to distinguish the two, both law and morality must be seen to be *integrated within an overall scheme of practical reason.* This might be clearer if we say something about our understanding of the category of practical reason in general, and on the differences between its identifiable components: the instrumental, the prudential, and the moral, before attempting to demarcate the latter from the legal.

Instrumental reason is the most basic form of practical reason in that it is concerned solely with the effective employment of means to the achievement of *given* ends. Issues of efficient employment of effective means suggest a slightly more complex dimension of the instrumental but remain a fairly uncontentious area of reasoning if, as well as *given ends*, we also have uncontentiously *given* criteria of what constitutes efficiency. *Prudential reason* is somewhat richer in conceptual content. It is about the instrumentally rational employment of means to ends constituted by what a person might subjectively define or value as being in his or her interests. These interests might or might not extend to, or coincide with, what other people consider to be in their own interests. Thus I act in a prudentially rational manner when I employ means which are conducive to, or consonant with, the fulfilment of what I take to be my own interests. *Morality* may be contrasted with this form of practical reasoning by suggesting that prudence is what I ought to do in my *own* interests, whereas morality is not only concerned with what means and ends I consider to be decent and acceptable in my own private

21

activities, but also extends to the similarly subjective area of how I consider I should treat *others*. This subjectivist view is not an entirely unreasonable understanding of the idea of morality; however, reflection on the possible scope of the relationship between prudential and moral reason has, historically, raised some strikingly more complex conceptions. For although morality can be defined in many ways—some of which may conveniently suit one argument rather than another—the logical problem of the justification of *ends* or goals which are not conveniently self-defined or *given* raises the question of the justification of *unconditional or categorical* values in general, and thus categorical and *other-regarding* values in particular. The 'other-regarding' dimension of the issue is, of course, crucial; but initially and more intractably it is the *categoricality* of practical prescription which causes the epistemological and thus the justificatory problem. This is best understood through an appreciation of the difficulties inherent in the attempt to manufacture general prescriptions from conceptions of prudential reasoning. Let us consider a couple of examples of this strategy.

In the attempt to avoid apparently insupportable categorical assertions of value in articulating what is held to be 'good' or 'right' or 'moral', putative justifications of normative prescriptions may appeal to prudential rationality. Prudence counsels that one ought to do x because x is a means to y, and that the achievement of y (as an end or goal) is in one's interests. If y is uncontentiously accepted, or can be convincingly demonstrated, as being in a person's (more precisely, an agent's) own interests, then the appeal to prudence is unproblematic. However, issues of value-judgement arise when prudence, rather than being merely self-defined or self-evidently accepted, is itself *prescriptively*, remotely and often counter-intuitively conceptualised as a set of interests which agents, to be 'prudent', ought to adopt. This approach becomes further implicated in value-judgement when the model or 'ideal-type' of prudential interest on offer posits all manner of ends (and consequently all manner of activities seen as 'acceptable' means to these ends) which agents *ought* to value *if* they understood what was genuinely constitutive of their genuine prudential interests. Hobbes' argument in *Leviathan* is one dramatic example of how the concept of prudence might be massively and, many have suggested, implausibly expanded in this way. So too are Rawls' and Gauthier's versions of contractarianism, and J.S. Mill's account of 'Utilitarianism'. [28]

But another way of conceiving of morality would be to begin from accepting that prudence is a valid and necessary form of

[28] It is not, of course, possible in a few sentences to do justice to these immense contributions to moral and political philosophy; but let us try and make a very general point about their respective orientations to the problem. Rawls (*A Theory of Justice* (Oxford University Press, Oxford, 1972, e.g. chap. 1) asks us to imagine that we might have been thrown into the world as different people located in other sets of circumstances—perhaps dramatically more difficult circumstances—from the ones we might inhabit now. He then suggests that our conceptions of prudent self-interest from these hypothetical perspectives be regarded as validly transferable, first, to the identity and the situation we, again hypothetically, possess in ignorance of our fate, and, finally, to the identity and situation we actually inhabit. This is an ingenious version of the maxim: *do as you would be done by*, allied to the persuasive suggestion that this is the safest option in an uncertain world—even if viewed *retrospectively* from a position of apparent security.

Gauthier's work (*Morals by Agreement* Clarendon Press, Oxford, 1986) presents a complex and impressive version of much the same thesis, the idea being that acting morally in acknowledging and honouring mutual agreements to promote the interests of others, in the statistical long run, is prudent. Thus, again, we are not so much offered a theory of morality as a theory of normatively enhanced prudence. This, we think, might also be attributed to Mill's strategy in *Utilitarianism* (H.B. Acton (ed.), London, Dent, 1972, chap. 1).

Mill begins by arguing the Epicurean case that there can be no good reasons for action other than the production of one's own happiness, but that happiness is subjectively interpreted and diversely experienced. He then tries to show that *real* (as opposed to merely subjective) happiness involves the appreciation of philosophy, great literature, art, and in addition, a keen sensitivity to the flourishing and happiness of *other* people. This, in effect, characterises prudential reason as not only a justification of morality, but also a rational account of æsthetics. However, Mill's argument consists in the (possibly true) assertion that I will be *genuinely* happy only if I am good, and that being good entails, *inter alia*, a duty to promote the interests of others. Thus, again, we witness the attempt to show that prudence, taken as the instrumentally rational pursuit of *self-defined* interests (generically, 'happiness'), coincides with a favorable disposition to the interests of others).

practical reasoning, but that the *logically* (not morally) unavoidable requirement to *universalise*, in a *social* context, valid prudential precepts of prudence synthesised in an *individual* context, might modify the actual content of, and our understanding of, prudential rationality. That is, prudence appears as severely circumscribed in that there might be reasons intrinsic to it which demonstrate that I *unconditionally* or, as we have said, *categorically* ought to take into account and sometimes *prioritise* the interests of *others* when I act in a way which appears to be straightforwardly antithetical to what I take to be my interests. This type of argument, broadly Kantian and influentially developed by Gewirth,[29] begins from prudence and tries to show that there *necessarily* arises from it categorical, overriding and other-regarding reasons for action which must condition what, rationally, I take to be valid prudential reasoning. This approach, then, makes a distinction between, on the one hand, subjective and arbitrary declarations of self-interest and, on the other, the rational prudential will.[30] We might note, then, that whereas the earlier examples acknowledge only the validity of either the purely subjective, or the *normatively enhanced* prudential will, this view seeks to portray 'other-regarding'—i.e. moral—reasoning as a related, yet distinct *and superior*, form of practical reason in that prudence modified by rationality becomes subordinate to morality. It is this latter view which, we suggest, is the most urgent object of moral inquiry, and one which gives rise to the possibility of conceiving of legality as the most complex stage in an *integrated continuum of practical reason*. This we will try to explain.

Our first take on morality was to suggest that it is subjective and voluntaristic in the sense that each individual is free to

[29] See e.g. Kant, Immanuel, *The Critique of Practical Reason* (Lewis White Beck (trans.), Bobbs-Merrill, Indianapolis (1956), 36–40; Gewirth, A., *Reason and Morality* (Chicago University Press, Chicago, 1978), chap. 1; and most importantly Beyleveld, D., *The Dialectical Necessity of Morality* (Chicago University Press, Chicago, Ill., 1991), esp. on 'The Logical Principle of Universalisation' (LPU), chap. 3, 52ff.

[30] In Kant, respectively *Wille* as opposed to *Wilkür*: see Kant (n. 2 *supra*) at 11–14.

adopt, select or reject values and prescriptions as a matter of personal whim. Thus there are no compelling reasons for acting in accordance with the interest of others that do not happen to coincide with one's own interest or preferences. The second, what we have referred to as a theory of normatively enhanced prudence, although admittedly more thoughtful, seems to endorse a similar view. However, the third approach to the problem seeks to demonstrate that there are compelling practical reasons which sometimes, and in some circumstances, *rationally oblige* agents to subordinate or modify their prudential interests to take into account the interest of *others*.

Let us not argue at this point about the relative merits of these contrasting views, but on the basis of adopting one or another of them let us consider the following, inevitable questions, accepting as we must that an extreme form of moral subjectivism might reject their relevance *tout court*. The first would be how might we *rationally* structure our relations with each other to reflect these general understandings of the principles of practical reason and interest. The second: what would be the *practically rational response* to the problem of disagreement or uncertainty in respect of the interpretation or application of these principles, or a refusal on the part of some to acknowledge the general principles *per se*. These unavoidable questions constitute the aspect of practical reason we regard as the dimension of the legal. It is thus perfectly plain how completely the conception of the relationship between prudential and moral reason determines the conceptualisation of the essential nature and function of the legal enterprise.

In so far as any conception of morality presupposes some form of relationship to prudential and instrumental rationality, the legal, as it relates to all three from the point of view of institutionalisation and enforcement, is a conceptually related aspect of practical reason, and thus, demonstrably, there exists a 'necessary connection' between law and morality. This point, however, is, or should be, so obvious as to be of little consequence. The important and difficult questions revolve around whether prudence implies a sovereign sphere of moral reason, and whether moral reason thus *directly* and 'naturally' (as opposed to 'artificially') conceived can survive the dramatic metamorphosis of institutionalisation in any form determinate enough to allow it to be identifiably—we shall say transparently—applied *indirectly* in the form of authoritatively enforceable norms. If it can, then legality *ought* to aspire to these exacting standards of practical reason, and in so far as it strives optimally and openly to do this, then the authority of law is a moral authority and legal obligation can be seen as a form of moral obligation.

Evaluation and Description

In the light of what has been said immediately above, our third source of dissatisfaction concerns the perennially recurrent strategy adopted by those who, although acknowledging the important role of morality and moral reasoning in jurisprudential matters, do not wish to embroil themselves in evaluative or prescriptive debate but wish merely to 'study law as it is, and not as it ought to be'. This phrase has been uttered by some of the most influential and assiduous of legal philosophers—and for very good reasons. However, it is often enthusiastically reiterated and endorsed for very bad reasons. Among those who do have a genuine methodological interest, this aspiration to confine oneself to the facts is, at best, a misunderstanding of the general problem of appropriating institutional phenomena in general for the purposes of social science. At worst, however, taken as an argument against the classical natural law position of *lex iniusta non est lex*, this pronouncement simply begs the question in that, in response to the thesis that rules cannot genuinely be regarded as laws unless they are morally valid, the reply amounts to nothing more than the banal observation that this argument must be false *because* there exist many 'laws' which are morally reprehensible. This is even more unsatisfactory when we reflect, in the light of our preceding remarks, upon what here might be intended by the idea of 'morality'. We attempt to make the appropriate methodological arguments in response to this in Chapter 3.

'Morality' or 'Democracy'?

Our fourth point concerns what has recently become an influential attempt to discredit natural law theory by contrasting morality with democracy. It rests on the assumption that moral reasoning undermines the legitimacy of a state in so far as legitimacy arises from democratic participation in the law-making process. The argument, simply put, is that once an elected and notionally representative body has issued law, then judges and officials should not be allowed to apply individually reasoned moral precepts in the ensuing interpretive (adjudicative) process. To do so, it is alleged, amounts to allowing those who apply the law the opportunity to insulate themselves from the influence of the democratic will and exploit the malleable nature of moral principles in the exercise of uncheckable discretion. Our critique in Chapter 4, particularly of Ingeborg Maus, leads us to reconsider the fundamentals of the political philosophy which seeks to relate legislative sovereignty to the will of the people.

Legal Validity and 'Legal Validity'

Our fifth and final point is perhaps closest to our central preoccupations. It is to note that curiously, and despite the existence of the notorious if infinitely ambiguous positivist/naturalist divide over the issue of the concept of law, or, more specifically, the concept of legal validity as it relates to the notion of legal obligation, contemporary legal philosophy as a whole is in fact rather comfortable with the assertion that there is some form of fundamental connection between law and morality. This, as we argued earlier, is almost unavoidable. However, as we noted in our remarks concerning ambiguity within jurisprudential discourses, this accommodation appears to extend to the idea that authentic natural lawyers might find agreement with archetypal legal positivists that there indeed exist immoral, yet 'legally valid', rules, thus demonstrating the 'separation', or what we referred to earlier as the 'autonomy', of law from morality. If, as

27

William Lucy puts it,[31] this *entente cordiale* is to constitute a plat-form for the future of legal theory, then in our view the notions of legal validity and legal autonomy ought to be re-examined. To this end we turn, in the following chapter, to a consideration of the reasons why this unlikely compromise appears, *prima facie*, as a good idea.

[31] See (n. 23 *supra*).

2

The Good Sense of Legal Positivism

There exist, as we noted in Chapter 1, some complex variations of the foundational thesis of legal positivism. It is not our aspiration to give a comprehensive critical review of these various conceptions, or even to try to account for them. We do, however, need a working definition of *legal*, as opposed to other, and largely unrelated, forms of positivism, and in the following discussion we shall settle for a simple and broad notion of the parameters of legal positivism to which we think most proponents of it can subscribe. It is important, however, to emphasise that our arguments do not stand or fall with our definition of legal positivism. We are in the business of exploring and articulating a more comprehensive conception of the legal enterprise, not knocking down one or several versions of legal positivism. Our intentions in this regard should not arouse too much suspicion: we are, let us recall, merely attempting to show why legal positivism is, *prima facie*, an attractive option.

The general thesis of legal positivism can be explained as the idea that a valid legal order can exist in so far as it meets certain pragmatic, systemic and procedural criteria—even if its norms are thought to be, or are, morally deficient. Jeremy Waldron, in his essay 'The Irrelevance of Moral Objectivity'[1] characterises legal positivism in the following way:

> According to that conception, law can be understood in terms of rules or standards whose authority derives from their provenance in some human source, sociologically defined, and which can be identified as law in terms of that provenance. Thus statements about

[1] Waldron, Jeremy in George, R.P. (ed.), *Natural Law Theory: Contemporary Essays* (Clarendon Press, Oxford, 1992), 160.

what the law is—whether in describing a legal system, offering legal advice, or disposing of particular cases—can be made without exercising moral or other evaluative judgement.

It is, then, characteristic of legal positivism to suggest that law inhabits a sphere of practical reason which, in some sense, is autonomous from morality. Thus we may say that legal positivism endorses what Gerald Postema calls 'the Autonomy Thesis'.[2]

The 'Autonomy' of Law

The descriptive and explanatory basis of this extremely important idea is common to most, if not all, sociological, legal and political theory in that it proceeds from the assumption of the problematic nature of achieving and maintaining a viable quantum of co-ordinatated order and intersubjective agreement in any significant human group. The Autonomy Thesis—henceforth, AT—has three logically indispensable, and logically interrelated components: the Limited Domain Thesis, the Pre-Emption Thesis, and the Source Thesis. These three components (sub-theses) express the demands of the AT in that 'law', i.e. a body of 'autonomous' norms, operates in a limited domain of practical reason common to officials and citizens alike; that these norms constitute *exclusionary*[3] reasons for action in that they preclude and override conflicting reasons or normative preferences outside the domain, and these, therefore *preemptive*, norms be *identifiable at source*[4] without recourse to

---

[2] Postema, Gerald, 'Law's Autonomy and Public Practical Reason' in George, R.P., *The Autonomy of Law: Essays on Legal Positivism* (Clarendon Press, Oxford, 1996), 79–119.

[3] By 'exclusionary' force, we mean that the rule contains a norm which is to be considered as a valid reason for action and which is to be held to exclude the adoption of, or preference for, other competing reasons for action.

[4] The idea of pre-emption is obviously related to the idea of exclusionary rules: they pre-empt certain motivations and exclude the related reasons for action outside the limited domain; the idea of non-moral identification of such rules is, of course, the generally Hartian idea of a rule of recognition. See Hart, H.L.A., *The Concept of Law* (Clarendon Press, Oxford, 1961), 92ff.

moral argument or political evaluations which might exist and function in various influential ways outside the limited domain. Once the legal order has been defined by the constituting sources, the agents of that order are not only positively provided with reasons to act in certain ways, but the legal norms, as identified through the 'source test', also, negatively, constitute a reason for *not acting* on certain other (i.e. competing) reasons.

In accordance with this, the *Leitmotif* of legal positivism can be seen as the aspiration to secure for law an independent sphere within the realm of practical reason, which primarily is a matter of attempting to seal off, at the foundational level, 'law' and legal discourse from 'morality' and moral discourse. Now, in order for legal positivism to make sense, it must be the case that it is possible to set up separate criteria for legal and moral validity (rightness, correctness or whatever) such that the former is decidable in isolation from the latter.

There is, of course, a plethora of opinion about what constitutes the right morality and the right moral answer to a particular social conflict. Furthermore, there is much debate in relation to how the moral should be delimited from the non-moral. The consequence of acknowledging this situation, as we will explain, is that it becomes a moral point in itself to transcend these controversies by creating a set of institutions (a state) whose agents can act with an authority and power in relation to societal rule and decision-making that override the unilateral claims of morality which are made by individual citizens or groups of citizens. The configuration of sovereignty, state and law in relation to 'the people' is a complex matter,[5] but for our purposes here we will assume a familiar model of 'representative' democracy.

The first principle of the state is that state regulation takes priority as against private regulation. The state is organised around the three logical phases of regulation, norm creation, norm application and norm enforcement, and the competence of the

[5] See Chap. 4 *infra*; also, e.g., *cf.* Kant, Immanuel, *The Metaphysics of Morals* (Mary Gregor (trans.) Cambridge University Press, Cambridge, 1996), 90–113; Rousseau, J.J., *The Social Contract and Discourses* (G.D.H. Cole (trans.), Dent, London, 1983), book 2, 182–205.

state is usually written into a document—a written constitution—that sets out the most important ground rules of the particular state. In order that the representatives of the state do not exploit the competence they have been given, a number of control functions have been set up. These control functions vary from state to state, but among the most common are: general elections, a certain institutional separation of the three phases of regulation, ministerial responsibility (political and legal), a parliamentary ombudsman, constitutional courts, judicial control, appeal, pardon, and so on. The Autonomy Thesis (AT) constitutes, in a sense, a supplement to these control functions in that it introduces a certain constraint in relation to *institutionalised* norm application. This constraint consists first and foremost of a delimiting of the *sources* from which those who apply norms (judges, officials or otherwise) may draw their normative concepts. A judge that operates within such a system cannot base his decisions on his own personal conception of justice or morality. Instead he must follow the rules of the system, and apply the norms which have been generated through the norm-creating processes of that system. Both Hans Kelsen and H.L.A. Hart have contributed significantly to the understanding of how the idea of the AT works in the legal mind. Kelsen's *Grundnorm*, which is the product of a neo-Kantian analysis of legal reasoning, expresses the foundational norm-logic of such a system. Hart's 'Rule of Recognition' adds to Kelsen's formal analysis a sociological-linguistic explanation of the practical deliberations of the lawyer at work in the 'autonomous' or morality-free zone of law. [6]

Taking a wider, politico-sociological, view of the AT, we will show that it amounts to a compelling and persuasive reconstruction or, as Postema says, a 'creation myth' of the idea of a legal system. It captures the deceptively simple insight that legality

[6] Kelsen, Hans, *The Pure Theory of Law* (California University Press, Berkeley, Cal., 1967), 198–201; see Beyleveld, Deryck, and Brownsword, Roger, *Law as a Moral Judgment* (Sweet and Maxwell, London, 1986), chap. 6; also generally Paulson, Stanley L. and Paulson, Bonnie Litschewski (ed.) *Normativity and Norms* (Clarendon Press, Oxford, 1998). *Re* Hart, see n. 4 *supra*.

arises as a special and independent sphere of practical reason in response to the co-ordinatory and regulatory tasks arising from social complexity, ensuing value-pluralism, and the debilitating condition—which we explain below—of moral 'disenchantment'. In transcending the context of social and political discourses of morality and interest in order to regulate and co-ordinate this sphere of conflictual interaction, the normative autonomy of the special 'limited domain' allegedly acquires a form of authoritative dispensation from the traditional need to legitimise social action through moral principles. Reciprocally, it seems, this provides the addressee of norms issuing from this autonomous domain with practical and *exclusionary*—but not necessarily moral—reasons for compliance. If autonomy is equated with legality, it thus provides the addressee of a norm with an obligation to obey which is neither (necessarily) a form of subjective personal or objective-natural morality, a function of traditional or cultural habit or loyalty, nor mere coercion backed by threat of harm. Thus, it seems, the AT provides a solution to the problem of characterising and grounding a form of obligation which, in Chapter 1, we located as existing between less problematic and less comprehensive polar forms of obligation.[7]

The AT, in our view, presents a rich and compelling ontological base from which to theorise the practical reasonableness of institutions and their relationship to individual and group striving. Thus, social theory and political philosophy are not so much a detour for legal theory as appropriate points of departure in the attempt to theorise a particular and complex form of normativity; a form which is acutely concerned with practical reasons for compliance. In subsequent chapters we will take a closer look at the normative origins of the AT but for the moment let us note that its *rationale* accords with the idea that law serves the purpose of establishing and securing determinate criteria of justice and equality of right, and of positing normative standards which allow for judgments that are independent of the individual citizens' and authorities' personal and particular sense of justice.

---

[7] See Chap. 1, n. 3, 4 *supra*.

These, it seems, are the ultimate and general goals and values of a lawful polity, but in order to achieve them there remains the practical task of setting up a framework of public practical reasoning and establishing mechanisms for some form of co-ordination of social interaction. In Kantian (and pre-Kantian[8]) terms, these aspirations can be achieved only by the formation of an 'artificial', publicly accessible, univocal standard of right which implies that these public institutions must be set up and granted authority to overrule the unilateral moral or value judgements of individual citizens.[9] In addition, such institutions are viable only if manifestly authoritative, wherefore the system must claim obedience and must have the necessary means to sustain and uphold such obedience. The operative assumption behind the AT, then, is that social complexity, moral diversity and interest-plurality are the source of the fundamental societal problem to which legality—as a source of settled norms—is a response. This means that we must eschew moral rationality as a criterion of legality in that morality can only be conceived as reproducing the destabilising indeterminacy of the pre-legal condition.

Indeterminacy and conflictual value-plurality are not exclusively a property of advanced modern societies, but they are a fundamentally valid characterisation of modernity in that not only is there an intensity of interest differentiation, but also a condition of what Weber called '*disenchantment*'. This is the term which Weber used to refer to a condition in which there exists an ethos of resignation to the idea that rational thought is incapable of supplying criteria for our choice between values. In this context, legal positivism can be seen as progressive in that, ideal-typically, it represents an attempt to confront the emergence of dynamic interest and value-pluralism in the recognition

[8] Both Coke and Hobbes, over a century before, use the expression.

[9] By 'unilateral' we have in mind Kant's opposition between the individual determination of right and the collective (omnilateral) or institutionalised determination of right. See Kant (n. 5 *supra*) §46; and also Waldron, Jeremy, 'Kant's Legal Positivism' (1996) 109 *Harvard Law Review* 1535 at 1558. See our discussion in Chap. 4 *infra*. and in 'Idealism for Pragmatists' *Archiv für Recht und Sozialphilosophie* 4/99.

that the only basis available for legitimacy is through an appeal to the need for broad social co-ordination combined with the accountability and predictability of 'legal' procedures[10] In the light of this we can see clearly why legal positivists propound not only the possibility, but the *desirability* of the separation of law and morals.

Morally Sensitive Legal Positivism

However, it is not necessary to subscribe to any form of moral non-cognitivism to see the logic of securing 'the autonomy' of institutionalised dispute-resolution procedures (law) from the sphere of political and personal morality. Clearly, one might hold strong moral opinions or even claim access to objectivity in moral reasoning, yet still hold the view that it is the very autonomy of law from this sphere of potential disagreement that is the precondition of its effective operation. This seems even more attractive if we can have it all ways by at once embracing the thesis of law's autonomy from morality such that legal validity (and thus, implied authority and obligation) need not be tied to moral validity, yet simultaneously, as Herbert Hart was almost tempted to suggest, adopt one of the 'great battle cries' of legal positivism: that some 'laws' are too iniquitous to be applied and obeyed.[11] This position, however, as we shall presently see, is extremely problematic. This positivistic, yet morally sensitive, opinion is carefully and impressively articulated by Radbruch. In his *Rechtsphilosophie* he

[10] For Weber's views on the idea of legitimacy in the modern state see Bendix, Reinhard, *Max Weber: An Intellectual Portrait* (University of California Press, Berkeley, Cal., 1977), chap. XIII, which points particularly to Weber, Max, *The Theory of Social and Economic Organisation* (Oxford University Press, New York, 1947), 154–6; and also his *Staatssoziologie* (Dunker and Humboldt, Berlin, 1956), 99. An important discussion is to be found in Habermas, Jurgen, *The Theory of Communicative Action* (Heinemann, London 1984), i. 256–71, and similarly in relation to Weber's ethical ideas, in Brubaker, Rodgers, *The Limits of Rationality* (George Allen & Unwin, London, 1984), 61–114.

[11] See Hart (n. 4 *supra*), 203.

explains why a positivistic caution about tying legal validity to morality appears as the best option[12]:

No doubt, if the purpose of the law and the means necessary to attain it could be known with scientific clarity, the conclusion would be inescapable that Natural Law, once it was scientifically recognized, must extinguish the validity of positive law deviating therefrom, just as the disclosure of truth must extinguish the exposed error. The validity of demonstrably wrong law cannot conceivably be justified. However, any answer to the question of the purpose of law other than by enumerating the manifold partisan views about it has proved impossible—and it is precisely on the impossibility of any Natural Law, and on that alone, that the validity of positive law must be founded.

The point seems to be that if we were to insist that legal validity depends on moral validity, and accept that morality is disputed, not only among laymen, but even among moral philosophers, the notion of legal validity becomes relativised to opinion and susceptible to indeterminate dispute. If legality is a means to some form of normative stability and predictability, legal validity cannot rationally be constructed in so fragile a manner. Thus, moral dispute must be excised from discourse wherever it threatens this stability. This, however, is not an abrogation of reason and right, but an attempt to face the responsibilities of justifying and legitimising the enforcement of 'legal' norms in the face of philosophical difficulties. There is, then, in this zone of apparent paradox, a chance for *rapprochement* between broadly positivistic and naturalistic opinion.

In attempting to explain the nature of this reconciliation, Radbruch reflects on the relationship between science and truth. Science is an activity of fallible human beings, and Radbruch rightly observes that we should be wise to remain aware of the distinction between science and truth.[13] The difference is that

[12] See Radbruch, Gustav, in Wilk, K. (trans.), *The Legal Philosophies of Lask, Radbruch, and Dabin* (Harvard University Press, Cambridge; Mass., 1950), 116. See generally Section 2, 'Legal Philosophy as the Evaluating View of Law', especially at 57ff.

[13] *Ibid*, 50.

the science of an age embraces not only its achievements, but also its failures and errors. When a scientific error is taken to belong to science despite its failure to convey the truth, it is because the human effort that produced the error genuinely and systematically aimed at or pursued the truth. This distinction, says Radbruch, should illuminate our thinking about the relationship between law and justice in that the meaning of law is to serve justice, and just as science may fail in its quest for truth, so too may law fail in its quest for justice. However, in order to recognise a rule as a legal rule, we have to be able to see it as a rule which genuinely aims at justice; just as we can recognise an activity as science only if the systematic purpose of that activity is an attempt to convey the truth. This is an important observation, not least because it resonates powerfully with influential and parallel views concerning the nature of science as opposed to pseudo-science. Karl Popper's 'falsificationist' thesis readily springs to mind in that, in addition to examining the problem of reconciling predictive and general theory with inductive reasoning, it suggests that the idea of all science relies heavily on the notion of good faith.[14] But having made this important point, Radbruch stresses that it is not possible to derive, from the notion of justice, legal rules of a definite content. Justice, Radbruch explains, is simply the demand that equals be treated equally, different ones differently according to their differences. This gives rise to two points. The first is that the concept of justice leaves open the most important questions, namely, *whom* to consider equal or different, and *how* to treat them.[15] This is problematic because these questions can be answered only by answering the further question—to put it in its most simple form—of what is morally right and wrong.

There exists, says Radbruch, at all levels of society a permanent debate about not only the individual, social and economic ends in question, but also the most expedient or appropriate way

<hr/>

[14] See, for example, Popper, K., *Conjectures and Refutations* (Routledge & Kegan Paul, London, 1963), 253–80, on induction; on reason and democracy, see 347–77.

[15] Radbruch (n. 13 *supra*).

of achieving certain stipulated ends. Different theories of law thus comprehend the complexities and priorities of individual and institutional aspirations and strategies in different ways. However, on any account of the good society, or, let us note, any account of a *modus vivendi* based on abandoning the quest for the good society, some form of order is required. This is not achievable in a constant state of confusion and disagreement about norms and values. Some 'certainty' or stability in normative life is required. The second and related point is that, even on the assumption that the difficult questions of moral rightness cannot be answered, we must note that any account of what is required in order for a rule to be seen as formally just (i.e. 'just' in Radbruch's sense), must rely on some notion of equality. And if this is not to be seen as a completely empty, purely formal requirement, we must strive to ensure that the notion of justice approaches some *substantial* coherence throughout the whole of the legal system.

Now, in order to present what might well be characterised as an attempt to formulate a morally conscientious legal positivism, Radbruch introduces us to a trinity of values[16]: law as justice (*Gerichtigkeit*), purpose (*Zweckmässigkeit*) and an authoritative and stable certainty or predictability of norms (*Rechtssicherheit*). These values, if not mutually exclusive, lie in obvious tension. On the one hand there is a need for cohesion and some form of intersubjectively acceptable (authoritative) order which can create a settled or predictable framework in this condition of moral and political diversity. On the other, such an order, if it is to aspire to legal validity, must remain, at least in some minimal sense, in accord with moral rightness. In the light of Radbruch's thoughts on the idea of striving, it seems that legal positivists and natural lawyers can come close to agreement here. It seems eminently reasonable to suppose that the attempt to 'do our moral best' in such circumstances is the optimal solution. What this involves is a matter of attempting to weigh conflicting interests and to interpret the law in a way which makes it as coherent as

---

[16] Radbruch (n. 13 *supra*).

possible with the most basic of the underlying (implicit) value principles. Thus, if moral validity were to mean 'doing one's moral best to be reasonable' and legal validity rested necessarily upon this condition; and, further, if legal obligations were seen to arise in relation to practical reasonableness; and if it were recognised that legality was about striving towards moral rightness under difficult conditions as opposed to instantiating it infallibly, then, it seems, there would be little or perhaps no basis for argument between legal positivists and natural lawyers. We are inclined to think that, at its best, legal positivism does implicitly subscribe to these suppositions—which is different from supposing or pointing to actual agreement on the matter. We take up, therefore, some of the objections to what we believe, all things considered, is the best interpretation of legal positivism.

Problems Ahead

First, we must note that Radbruch himself seems to give up his tripartite scheme of legal values when it comes down to the uncomfortable business of judging. Instead he emphasises legal certainty as the only value the judge should consider. But this leads to a version of legal positivism which is far more difficult to reconcile with a morally sensitive or legal idealist position, and we therefore anticipate that proponents of this more rigid version of legal positivism might object to our ecumenical call. But let us for a moment suppose that a comprehensive concept of law must acknowledge that legal validity and, hence, legal obligation, is determined by an interplay between morality and certainty. Moral rightness is thus a relevant factor in relation to the application of legal rules and ought to be considered as such by anyone who makes decisions in law. The problem with this, as we have seen, is that it seems to presuppose the possibility of knowing a right answer to the question of what the substantive purpose or end of law is in terms of morally right rules. This we have already recognised as fundamentally problematic, and we are not entirely unsympathetic with Radbruch when he says that '[i]f no one is able to determine what is just, somebody must lay

39

down what is to be legal'.[17] However, let us note that Radbruch's legal positivism becomes rigid at the point where he—perhaps despairingly—concedes defeat and thus prescribes that judges ought to be devoted, at least in professional life, only to the value of certainty (*Rechtssicherheit*)[18]:

> It is the professional duty of the judge to give expression to the intended validity of the statute, to sacrifice his own sense of what is right, in deference to the authoritative command of the law, to ask only what is legal, never whether it is also just . . . We despise the parson who preaches in a sense contrary to his conviction, but we respect the judge who does not permit himself to be diverted from his loyalty to the law by his conflicting sense of justice.

The bottom line of adjudication is that the judge (and presumably other officials) must give full priority to the value of certainty. There can be no dispute that certainty and predictability are important values—in fact, essential components of the analysis of the concept of law and legal validity. These values must be respected by anyone who has authority to make decisions in law. But it is of great moment in the analysis of the problem in hand to announce that we must let the moral requirement slide in order to give absolute priority to the value of legal certainty (*Rechtssicherheit*). Radbruch's struggle with this dilemma has already been comprehensively analysed by Stanley Paulson.[19] Our interest, however, lies not so much with Radbruch's analysis *per se* but rather, that before we can respond to the tensions between the values of legal certainty and moral rightness, two things must be made clear. The first is that the value of legal certainty is a relative one: it makes sense only in the context of other values, institutions and attitudes. In order to maintain its strength and immediate appeal, this context must be seen to be not entirely unjust and immoral. Secondly, it is a

[17] Radbruch (n. 13 *supra*) 117.

[18] *Ibid.*

[19] See Paulson, Stanley L., 'Radbruch on Unjust Laws: Competing Earlier and Later Views?' (1995) 15 *Oxford Journal of Legal Studies* 489; and 'Lon. L. Fuller, 'Gustav Radbruch and the "Positivist" Theses' in (1994) 13 *Law and Philosophy* 313–59.

mistake to assume that it is possible to find satisfactory answers to hard questions of law only if we ask 'what is legal, never whether it is also just'. To appreciate these points more fully we must take a closer look at the political philosophy of constitutionalism and at the logic of legal interpretation. We will do so in what we take to be an argument in favour of a concept of law which attempts to integrate the conflicting values of legal certainty and moral rightness.[20]

Legal Validity?

Before we can proceed, however, we must respond to a development in recent legal theory which appears to aspire to a condition of integration in this regard. For it is now true to say that modern legal positivists can and do admit that there is in some sense a 'necessary connection' between law and morality. Furthermore, and conversely, it is also the case that at least one influential proponent of what might be thought to be legal positivism's antithesis, i.e. the theory of natural law, concedes that there are immoral, yet 'legally valid', rules.[21] This state of affairs, ironically, could be seen as the beginning of a theoretical advance towards the effective dissolution of the argument between legal positivism and natural law and to offer the basis of a non-relativist solution to the justificatory problems of rationality, morality, validity and obligation. Unfortunately more problems than solutions seem to grow out of what William Lucy refers to as an *'entente cordiale'*. Let us recap briefly before considering the details of it.

We began by examining the urge among legal positivists to stress the importance of establishing an artificial sphere for legal reasoning—a sphere which has autonomy in relation to moral reason—hence, the autonomy thesis (AT)—and we found that

[20] See our discussions in Chaps. 5 and 6 *infra*.

[21] See Lucy, William, 'Natural Law Now' (1993) 56 *Modern Law Review* 745–60, where he points to the dubious foundations of the *'entente cordiale'* between Hartian Legal Positivism (as represented by Neil MacCormick) and Aquinian Natural Law (as represented by John Finnis).

this urge was based on the assumption that there was no generally accepted method whereby claims to moral rightness might be verified or falsified: moral disagreement exists, hence, law must be introduced. For if what is morally right cannot be settled, then the law must lay down what in practice ought to be right. This requirement to rise above the problematic nature of moral reasoning is crucial for the legal enterprise. But, as Radbruch also pointed out, law cannot be entirely severed from morality. Law arises from moral conflict, and in this sense it must *somehow* be conceived of as a moral phenomenon; but must we necessarily characterise its modes of internal justification as moral: for example, is legal validity a form of moral validity? A failure to respond in precise terms to this question could lead to obfuscation in another: that is, how, precisely, ought one to relate to the role of morality in legal reasoning? Our own attempt to provide an approach to this last question will appear in Chapters 5 and 6. But for the remainder of this chapter we shall turn to the nature of the compromise between positivism and naturalism which we find in MacCormick and Finnis.

'Technical' Legal Validity?

This new common ground arises from the idea that it is possible to isolate a 'technical' concept of legal validity. Thus these two writers appear to find some utility in establishing a separation between the concept of legal validity 'in the technical sense' and the moral duty to obey the law. Thus legal validity and moral obligation are not seen as interrelated concepts. MacCormick, endorsing Finnis' formulation of this distinction in the latter's *Natural Law and Natural Rights* and, more recently, in an influential collection of essays on 'autonomy' edited by R.P. George,[22] says[23]:

[22] Finnis, John, *Natural Law and Natural Rights* (Clarendon Press, Oxford, 1980); George, R.P., *The Autonomy of Law: Essays on Legal Positivism* (Clarendon Press, Oxford,1996).

[23] Maccormick, Neil, '*The Concept of Law* and the Concept of Law' in George (n. 22 *supra*), 163–93.

Validity in this [technical] sense has to do with the observance of proper procedures by persons having appropriate competence. Of course, there may be legislation which falls far short of or cuts against the demands of justice. The validity of the relevant statutory norms as members of the given system of law is not as such put in doubt by their injustice. The legal duties they impose, or the legal rights they grant, do not stop being genuinely legal duties or legal rights in virtue of the moral wrongfulness of their imposition or conferment. They are, however, defective or substandard or corrupt instances of that which they genuinely are—laws, legal duties, legal rights.

MacCormick continues:

This corruption or defectiveness does indeed weaken, and in grave cases simply negates, any moral case for obedience (to laws or duties) or respect (for rights). In being a defective law, an unjust enactment is, in a practical moral perspective, at best defectively obligatory, whether or not in the perspective of legal analysis it is a valid imposition of legal obligation.

There are several problem with this. The first is that MacCormick (and Finnis) isolates the value of observing 'proper procedures by persons having appropriate competence' to the sphere of law, and the substantive value of the regulatory instrument in question to the sphere of morality. But this distinction cannot be consistently maintained. Procedure is relevant for the evaluation of both the legal and the moral legitimation of any decision in law. It is true, of course, that procedure does not, in and of itself, secure substantial moral rights, but that is not the issue. The point is that considerations of procedure, competence, and so on become morally important in their own right. Therefore, procedural legitimation cannot be seen as an autonomous legal (technical) form of legitimation separate from general moral reasoning. Thus, at least from a moral point of view, the main concern will be with how much weight should be attributed to following legal procedures, and how much should be attributed to basic moral rights. This problem of weight of course, does not present itself in simple terms. Often (and it is important to point this out in relation to MacCormick and Finnis), the problem arises as a question of legal interpretation, either in relation to the abstract meaning of the right in question or in relation to the question of how far and in what way this right should be applied to the particular case in hand.[24]

The second problem relates to the notion of obligation. MacCormick is happy to emphasise his agreement with Finnis (and, originally, Aquinas) on two important points: one is that 'an unjust law is no longer legal but rather a corruption of law'; and the second is that 'this is not a thesis about the validity of law in its technical sense', for validity in this technical sense has merely to do with 'the observance of proper procedures by persons having appropriate competence'. But the consequence is that legal validity in this technical sense becomes separated from the concept of and, thus, the *issue* of, legal obligation. On this view, saying that a legal rule is valid in the technical sense says nothing about whether or not it should be obeyed. But this is problematic, for on this view, rules gives no guidance to practical reason. This is an important point, because the purpose of the AT from which all legal theory in this vein springs is to give *exclusionary* reasons which can work as guides for practical reason. Joseph Raz is especially informative on this point.[25] But by cutting free from moral reasoning a purely technical concept of legal validity, one in fact undermines the justificatory basis of the normative logic of the very idea of the autonomy of law. We end up with a concept of legal validity which has precisely the opposite effect, namely, that it has no authority to guide. By sealing off the concept of legal validity from practical and moral obligation, the concept of validity becomes empty. This is precisely the problem Fuller pointed out in his response to Hart in the Harvard Law Review 1958. Fuller says[26]:

> I hope I am not being unjust to Professor Hart when I say that I can find no way of describing the dilemma as he sees it but to use some

[24] We discuss this in some detail in Chap. 6 *infra*.

[25] See Raz, Joseph, *The Authority of Law* (Clarendon Press, Oxford, 1979), chap. 1.

[26] Fuller, Lon. L., 'Positivism and Fidelity to Law—A Reply to Professor Hart' (1958) *Harvard Law Review* 630–72 at 656.

such words as the following: On the one hand, we have an amoral datum called law, which has the peculiar quality of creating a moral duty to obey it. On the other hand, we have a moral duty to do what we think is right and decent. When we are confronted by a statute we believe to be thoroughly evil, we have to choose between those two duties.

If this is the positivist position, then I have no hesitancy in rejecting it. The 'dilemma' it states has the verbal formulation of a problem, but the problem it states makes no sense. It is like saying I have to choose between giving food to a starving man and being mimsy with the borogroves. I do not think it is unfair to the positivistic philosophy to say that it never gives any coherent meaning to the moral obligation of fidelity to law. This obligation seems to be conceived as *sui generis*, wholly unrelated to any of the ordinary, extra-legal ends of human life. The fundamental postulate of positivism—that law must be strictly severed from morality—seems to deny the possibility of any bridge between the obligation to obey law and other moral obligations. No mediating principle can measure their respective demands on conscience, for they exist in wholly separate worlds.

The point is that, if legal validity has nothing to do with legal obligation, and if legal obligation has nothing to do with practical (including moral) reason, then what, if anything, is at stake in the determination of the concept of law? Unless there is a genuine source of anxiety and reluctance about admitting something like: 'a rule is rightly acknowledged as valid law, and consequently should be accepted as rightly enforced and obeyed, only if it is morally acceptable', then it seems that nothing much turns on this novel compromise between MacCormick and Finnis. No problems whatsoever concerning the relationship between law and morals are solved by stipulatively redefining 'legal validity' as a non-moral, and ultimately nonpractical, issue. But what we suspect here is that the issue of obligation is implicitly being referred to some background notion of social or functional necessity—where an authoritative terminus of argument appears as a necessary means to some overall social goal. This, of course, requires us to relate and integrate the concept of *valid legal form* to the moral *substance* of the alleged goals which, effectively, are doing the justificatory work behind the facade of 'technical' validity.[27]

Thirdly, and related to the two first points, MacCormick and Finnis seem to overlook the way in which legal validity 'in the technical sense' hinges on moral validity in the justificatory sense. If we were to ask for the value which lies behind the idea of maintaining a concept of legal validity which is detached from moral evaluation, we would probably be told that the function of the legal system is to supply society with positive authoritative reasons like legislative acts and court decisions. These reasons, although perhaps morally defective, are still relevant from a legal point of view as long as they have been generated in accordance with the rule of recognition of that particular legal system from which they emanate. This is true and, moreover, these reasons are not relevant only from a legal point of view, but also from a moral point of view. There are two reasons why this is so. The first is the familiar Hobbesian point that in an imperfect world it is necessary, in order to avoid social chaos and to secure the value of legal certainty, to abide by authoritative reasons.[28] This answer shows us that 'authoritative' reasons, in the sense in which authority is underpinned by the value of *Rechtssicherheit*, are at their root, backed by a moral reason based on substantial moral principles which, if valid, are valid independently of any authoritative reasons in the form either of authoritative rule positing or authoritative decision making. Thus, in the last instance, authoritative reasons can remain only if they are backed by substantive reasons. The second reason relates to the fact that moral reasons are always constructed by fallible individual persons whose knowledge of the world and of themselves is always limited, wherefore, the solutions to the

[27] Although not specifically in relation to MacCormick, but Hart, we discuss this in Chap. 3 *infra* under the heading of *'Functionalist Jurisprudence?'*. In direct reference to Finnis, we discuss his background theory of obligation under the heading of *'Finnis:Legal Authority and Moral Incommensurability'* in Chap. 6 *infra*.

[28] Hobbes, T., *Leviathan* (C.B. McPherson (ed.), London, Pelican, 1968), Part II, chap. 26, 322.

many and varied types of societal problems may vary with the social situation of the person who is entrusted to make decisions in particular cases. By setting up a system of what is usefully and not perjoratively described as 'artificial' reasoning, based on autonomous authoritative reasons, and locking the individual decision-makers on to this system, one can secure a stable development enhanced by the channelled reasoning of the officials of the system, and thereby better overcome in the long run the limitations that accrue to the human capacity to reason. But this turns out, on closer inspection, to be insufficient as an argument for the thesis that it is possible to isolate a concept of legal validity 'in the technical sense'. Let us consider the following points suggested by Wibren van der Burg's distinction between 'law as a product' and 'law as a process'.[29]

The argument appears in two stages. In the first, Van der Burg shows how different theorists lay stress upon different aspects of the law, particularly when arguing about the question of what connection there is between law and morality. He suggests that we should be aware that there are several ways of approaching law, and that each way has its own incommensurable logic: that is, the internal consistency of a concept of law is relative to a particular model or paradigm of law. The models we are presented with are 'Law as a practice' and 'Law as a product'. The difference between these two models lies with the different ways in which they visualise the law: the 'product' model focuses on how law can be construed as a coherent body of norms, whereas the 'practice' model focuses on how the practices of interpretation and application shape the law. The differences between the two concepts are determined by their point of view. When taking the practice-oriented point of view, law is not something that exists entirely independently of the social processes through which the law is created. The social processes themselves and, particularly, the values inherent in these processes are part of the law itself. When taking the *product*-oriented point of view however, law consists of a number of

[29] Van der Burg, Wibren, 'Two Models of Law and Morality' forthcoming, in Aarnio, A. (ed.), *Associations* (1999), 3 (1), pp. 61–82.

statutes and precedents which contain the legal norms of a given society. The product model relies on some test for accepting material as being part of the law. In order to explain the relationship between the two models, Van der Burg invokes the physicist's problem of wave/particle duality.

In terms of the relationship between theoretical speculation and empirical experience, light can be modelled consistently *either* as a very small particle, or as a wave. Sometimes it shows characteristics which make the particle-model more suitable, while at other times, the wave-model seems more correct. This phenomenon, along with other notorious problems in particle theory, is often misleadingly and inappropriately employed to make all manner of claims about, for instance, the 'inherently contradictory nature of reality' and so on. However, the simple and apposite point being made here is that, in respect of a phenomenon such as light, as no unifying model appears to be logically available, the best option is to structure our practical and theoretical interests by alternating between the two models. Neither of the two models appears to be able to stand alone. For although they obey their own logic, they are not distinct: each model presupposes a reference to the other, yet appears incommensurable with the other. But let us not forget that, intuitively, and despite our ingenuity in generating the empirical 'facts', we are not readily disposed to accept (or genuinely comprehend) that light is, essentially and simultaneously, two contradictory phenomena rolled into one. Much the same is true, says Van de Burg, of the two models of law discussed hitherto.

On this background we can see that the basic idea behind the acknowledgement of legal validity 'in the technical sense' relies solely on the idea of 'law as a product'. Technical legal validity is used as an instrument to attach legitimation to the products of the legal system (i.e. the outcome of a process characterised by the 'observance of proper procedures by persons having appropriate competence'). But simultaneously, by describing the function of the legal system as one of supplying society with positive authoritative reasons like legislative acts and court decisions, the interpretive processes which takes place at all levels of the legal system are ignored. It is, of course, true that legal acts and court decisions are important as relevant sources of law: as authoritative reasons; but although they supply legal decision makers with authoritative reasons, they do not determine the outcome of the legal case at hand.[30] On this view, the process of interpretation is arbitrarily excluded from the concept of law. Only if we also include in our picture 'law as a practice' can we include the interpretive processes, and particularly the values inherent in these processes as part of the law itself. This brings us to the second stage of the argument.

Proponents of a morality-free concept of legal validity could argue in favour of their position, as we mentioned above, by suggesting that in setting up a system of artificial reasoning based on autonomous authoritative norms and locking the individual decision-makers on to this system, one could channel the reasoning of the officials of the system, whereby it would be possible to develop stable control of the limitations and instabilities of individual human reasoning. From this argument it follows that the more the legal interpretive processes can be controlled, the better. But how is such control of interpretation possible? If we conceptualise law as a *product*, and focus only on the sources of law, there will be too much leeway for manipulation, because we will have no criteria to guide us on the way from the letter of the law to the actual physical consequences of a legal decision. On the other hand, if we conceptualise law as a practice and focus only on the social processes, we risk ignoring the *substantial value* of the stabilising forces of legal formalism.[31] We must, then strive to formulate an integrated theory of law—a unified field in which we can explain and incorporate in a theory of legal obligation both the advantages of 'law as a product' and the advantages of 'law as a social practice'.

The issue for us, then, is to make legal formalism cohere with interpretive activity. The balancing of these two defining features of law must be both formally and substantially rational,

[30] See our discussion in Chap. 6 *infra* where we examine the moral complexity of legal form.

[31] See n. 29 *supra*.

and must, as Radbruch has shown us (a point to which we will return in some detail in our concluding chapter), be guided by the values which underpin the whole system. This, we think, is what presents the genuine challenge to jurisprudential thinking.

3
Legal Theory in Sociological Terms

In the preceding chapter we presented an analysis of the virtues and vices of separating law from morality. We explained how the problems of order, co-ordination and societal complexity have led legal theorists to conceive of law as a response to the practical-moral dilemmas involved in the construction of a general normative theory of adjudication. But some legal theories aspire to be value-neutral, in that they present an account of law which supposedly is purely descriptive. These accounts present law as a set of sociological facts and claim that these facts can be known without making or implying any moral judgement.

This descriptive approach to law echoes the Benthamite canon that we must separate the 'law as it is from the law as it ought to be'. In certain contexts of inquiry this is a perfectly reasonable aspiration; but as a comprehensive jurisprudential strategy, we will argue, it falls short of the minimum requirements of a genuinely sociological explanation of institutional phenomena. In this chapter we want to demonstrate how the jurisprudential debate is related to the discipline of sociology, and how social theory and, hence, legal theory in sociological terms cannot attain value-neutrality. First, however, we must identify and subsequently dispel certain confusions which arise when the language of the natural sciences and sociology meets the language of jurisprudence.

Terminology

Scope for misunderstanding lies with the term 'positivism'. Scientific positivism—which can be traced to the Baconian emphasis on empirical observation and the marking of regulari-ty (law-like connections) in nature—and in sociology perhaps most notably linked to Comte and Mill—is associated with a perhaps laudable and progressive distaste for superstition, 'animism' and speculative metaphysics in favour of testable or publicly verifiable hypotheses. Transferred to the social or 'moral' sciences this results in the attempt to transcend theolog-ical or overtly moralistic perspectives on the nature of society and history and to seek instead a unified scheme of scientific explanation. The project of developing a new language and a new framework of concepts appropriate to the presentation of historical and cultural phenomena is most familiar to us in the ninetenth-century terms of organic structure and the laws of evolutionary processes.

Durkheim and Marx are perhaps the most successful propo-nents of this perspective, and in terms of structuralist theories of societal development we are certainly indebted to them. However, there have been less successful attempts to imbue sociological and historical explanation with the rigour of the nat-ural sciences. These include the various late nineteenth-century Hegelianisms and psychologisms which became the target of Weber's seminal critique of method. Here, in what Weber calls the 'emanatism' of Roscher and Knies, we find the model of the hypothetico-deductive sciences and the nomological or 'cover-ing law' scheme of explanation grafted on to loosely disguised theological and romantic speculations. In response to this form of sociological positivism Weber counterposes the dual aspira-tions of, first, eschewing the mechanical apparatus of the nomo-logical or covering law approach to social science in favour of a more authentic and insightful grasp of the essential attributes of social phenomena, that is, to apprehend it 'meaningfully' as *pur-posive social action*; and secondly, to achieve this through an 'objective' or value-neutral (value-free) method. This alternative to positivism Weber referred to as the method of *verstehen*. On the basis of this understanding of the methodological controver-sy, we can identify three positions: (i) scientific positivism, understood as the hypothetico-deductive scheme held to be a description of the actual (and extremely successful) methods of the natural sciences; (ii) sociological positivism, understood as the acceptance of this account and the subsequent attempt to unify the sciences by advocating this approach as appropriate to historical and social phenomena; (iii) Weber's interpretive approach as the subsequent methodological synthesis which sought to expose and remedy the inadequacies and errors of the 'positivistic' attempt to 'unify' scientific method.

In particular, the project of unification exhibits two dramatic flaws: (a) its apparently disinterested, 'objective' and perhaps empirical pedigree as the basis of a rigorous natural science actually lends itself to quasi-religious, romantic-nationalist programmes of cultural ideology, and (b) its *empiricist* reliance on the 'observation' of law-like regularity (i.e. nomological explanation) fails to serve our urgent cognitive interests in relation to the purposive and 'meaningful' nature of history and society.

Thus we can contrast the interpretive method of Weber with the positivistic and unifying trend from Bacon to Comte to Mill and the Historical Economics of the early Heidelberg school. Logically, it would seem, Weber's approach is clearly *anti*-positivistic, however, usage of the term 'positivism' has gained much currency as a penumbral term to denote the particularly sociological aspiration to 'value-neutrality' in explanation and in concept formation. It is in this latter application that it has adhered to schools of legal theory which broadly subscribe to the thesis which denies the requirement of moral validity as a necessary or overwhelmingly important condition of legal validity—i.e. descriptive legal positivism. Clearly then, value-neutrality is one issue, and the dispute between empiricism (scientific positivism) and interpretivism another. That value-neutrality might appear as a feature of *both* methodological options offers scope for further ambiguity in the use of the term 'positivism'. Some legal theories, for example, have in fact adopted the ideal of a purely empirical science, and see it as their task to elaborate a methodology for legal science on this basis. Such is the approach of movements known as American Realism and later Scandinavian Realism, both of which treat legal phenomena as an unproblematically

53

accessible domain of fact. These movements both started on the basis of a sound scepticism towards legal formalism, and were fundamentally opposed to 'metaphysical' (by which they meant 'non-empirical') reasoning. This opposition runs from Holmes' dictum that '[l]aw is what judges do about disputes', to its most extreme form in Scandinavian Realism based on the epistemological theory of 'logical positivism'.[1] On this latter view, the study of law must be recognised as a science based on the empirically severe 'verification principle', and propositions about valid law must be seen as referring to value-neutral social facts. But, curiously, *legal* positivism in its most influential forms is clearly *anti-positivist* in terms of methodology. Let us consider this for a moment.

The classic case is, of course, Hart's critique of Austin's empiricist and behaviourist 'command theory of law' followed by his emphasis on the fecundity of adopting the 'internal point of view'—a strategy which is close to Weber's notion of the 'ideal-type'. We think in Hart's case that it is the anti-positivism in method which undermines the 'descriptive' legal positivism which is alleged to result from it.[2] In the light of these remarks, then, we might say that our central contention is that an empiricist or 'unified' scientific positivism is methodologically inappropriate, and that the interpretive or broadly Weberian approach cannot achieve value-neutral status. Thus we must be careful henceforth not to confuse or conflate, on the one hand,

[1] 'Logical positivism' was a 20th-century rehabilitation of Hume's empiricist doctrines and is perhaps most famously expounded and developed in Ayer, Alfred Jules, *Language Truth and Logic* (London, Pelican, 1946). He propounded the view that empirically unverifiable statements (other than simple tautologies) were, in fact, 'meaningless'. This view was encapsulated (problematically) in Ayer's formulation of the 'Verification Principle'. For an overview of American and Scandinavian Realism see Freeman, M.D.A. (ed.), *Lloyd's Introduction to Jurisprudence* (6th edn., Sweet and Maxwell, London, 1994), chaps. 8, 9.

[2] Hart says in the postscript to the 2nd edition of *The Concept of Law*: 'My account is descriptive in that it is morally neutral and has no justificatory aims: it does not seek to justify or commend on moral or other grounds the forms and structures which appear in my general account of law . . .' See Hart, H.L.A., *The Concept of Law* (2nd edn., Clarendon Press, Oxford, 1994), 249).

'positivism' as a methodological commitment to a model of unified scientific explanation, with what, on the other, is better
expressed as 'value-neutrality': the desire to remove moral
judgement from the ontological framework of social science.
The quickest way out of this is to note that 'scientific positivism',
'sociological positivism', 'value-neutrality' and 'legal positivism'
can be united only with much conceptual qualification.

The Case for the 'Ideal-type'

Our position is that scientific and/or sociological positivism (or
any of its behaviourist variants) rests on a methodological error.
Broadly, and from the viewpoint of a methodological framework, we agree with Weber (and, we might note, Finnis, Hart
and most other contemporary legal and social philosophers)
that, given our cognitive interests, an interpretive approach from
an 'internal' or 'practically reasonable' point of view is methodologically indispensable if we are to orientate ourselves systematically to the complexity of social phenomena. This is simply to
acknowledge that social action in general, and institutional
action in particular, is irreducibly purposive and must be apprehended as such. That is, we can make sense of social action only
in terms of a combination of what Weber refers to as 'axiology'
(the theory of the role of values in explanation) allied to 'tele-
ology' (the theory of the role of purposes in explanation). In
short, explanation of action must be couched in terms of norms
conceived as *means*, towards *ends* conditioned by values.
Furthermore, if we are to appropriate, for the purposes of
inquiry, large-scale institutional phenomena, such as the family,
gender, democracy, law and so on, we must abstract from the
infinite complexity and ambiguity of the actual processes of
social life and attempt to reconstruct heuristic models from the
empirical and rational resources at our disposal. The 'ideal-type'
seen as such a heuristic model is thus not a mere generalisation;
it is an instrumentally or perhaps prudentially rational (logically
ideal) reconstruction of an individual or institutional enterprise.
In other words, from general assumptions and investigations

concerning the actual or probable contexts of action and the basic axioms of successful prudential action, we believe that sociology must strive to offer an instrumentally rational general account of an institution in terms of an abstract purposive model; i.e. in terms of logically sound means to a coherently conceptualised end. Not surprisingly, it is the *ends* or ultimate purposes of law or democracy and so on, which, ideally conceived, provide us with much scope for disagreement. This is acutely obvious when the task is not so much reconstructing or divining suitable means to a given end, but rather being faced with the problem of positing a rational end *before* we can attempt to identify or interpret aspects of institutional activities conceived as means. Secondly, this does not mean (and neither does it follow from Weber's writings) that we should oppose a structuralist sociology, nor that we should reject the idea of structural determinism or structuralist accounts of 'function' or ideology, or assume that these aspects of ontology necessarily militate against the coherence of the idea of rational autonomy or, in a moral sense, free will and, hence, individual culpability.[3] Our discussion of Marx and Durkheim will explain our commitment in this regard. Conversely, neither does it follow that structuralist accounts of society as found in Marx or Durkheim are not accurately understood—in a Weberian sense—as *interpretive* accounts of the phenomena, or that they do not utilise or have recourse to the device of the ideal-type.[4]

An ideal-type of an institution merely attempts to give an account of the phenomenon in terms of its practical structure. To suggest that, say, capitalism is an institutionalised set of methods, ideologies (values) and procedures (means) to perpetuate class divisions and maximise surplus value (ends) is to offer what Weber understood by an ideal-type. Similarly, to suggest, for

[3] On this problem, see e.g. Beyleveld, Deryck, and Wiles, Paul, 'How to Retain Your Soul and be a Political Deviant' in Downes, D., and Rock, P. (eds.), *Deviant Interpretations* (Martin Robertson, Oxford, 1979), 123–43.

[4] For a discussion and further references to Giddens' views on the matter see Toddington, S., *Rationality, Social Action and Moral Judgment* (Edinburgh University Press, Edinburgh, 1993), n. 6 and text at pp. 202–4.

example, that gender roles, differences, and inequalities are necessary means to economic and psychological well-being within a wider structure of larger economic and sexual institutions is to attempt to disclose the instrumental rationale of these activities and practices in terms of a set of goals or deferred purposes. The fact that one might disagree about the nature of the characterisations on offer—that is, to disagree with the conception of the end or goal propounded in the analysis—and thus, in turn, object to the characterisation of the means, is not to deny that one has been offered *some* version of an ideal-type of the enterprises in question. However, to suggest that, for instance, Marx was mistaken in his characterisation of the ends of capitalism, or that Durkheim or Parsons misunderstood the *point*, the *rationale*, the *function*, of gender differences, is to embroil oneself in what could rapidly become a debate about the rationality of capitalism and gender in terms of *real* (as opposed to subjective or propagated or ideological) human interests—and real human interests are what people *would* want if they were possessed of the truth of their condition and a rational will. Let us pursue this line of thought.

Conceptualising Society

Let us consider the problem of conceptualising society for the purpose of any social theory. The point of departure, phenomenologically, is the individual attempting to make sense of his or her multi-dimensional relations with the natural world and the world of language mediated relations of, and with, other individuals. Broadly, we have a notion of a system of co-ordinated expectations which conditions the way we communicate, produce subsistence, relate sexually, apportion tasks, distribute resources and so on. This occurs in a physical, natural setting, of course, but, sociologically speaking, this set of *normative* relations constitutes the total social *environment* for action, and this idea is perhaps closest to what Durkheim, and later Parsons, intended by the notion of the social system or *structure*. Within the total social structure there are of course sub-structures or sub-systems, and the boundaries between various internal

systems and the total system-environment is a complex matter
and perhaps, ultimately a matter of cognitive orientation, if not
conceptual choice. But this problem applies to bio- and eco-sys-
tems equally, and should not be regarded as some drawback
peculiar to social theory.[5] But from the perspective of any particular individual or sub-group, all *other* individuals, sub-groups
and their purposes are part of this structured environment, this
network of constraints and channels, this inter-linking system of
obstacles and opportunities. There is, in actuality, a staggering
complexity to these relations, as well as the additional complexity of identifying functional units by reference to relevant sub-
structures or sub-*environments* within the total social structure.[6]
Theoretically, however, we must focus on the major features of
the societal landscape. These features appear as institutional
obstacles to certain forms of behaviour and the achievement of
certain purposes and, we must note, major sources of encouragement. In the sense that they are major and entrenched, they
are institutions. In the sense that they implicitly inhibit or
encourage particular ways of going about achieving particular
ends they are normative—they embody a standard of correctness or propriety. So, we are now talking about a system of
normative institutions which constitutes the environment of
social action. These institutions need not necessarily be conceived as being immutable, although from the point of view of
theory, and as a matter of fact, they are durable and effective.[7]

[5] There is an important discussion of these ontological issues in Parsons,
Talcott, 'The Present Status of "Structural-Functional" Theory in Sociology' in
Coser, Lewis A. (ed.), *The Idea of Social Structure* (Harcourt Brace Jovanovich,
New York, 1975), 67–85. Parsons also notes (at 72) that Durkheim's most devel-
oped views on the social structure are to be found in his later work, *The Elementary
Forms of the Religious Life* (Trans. Joseph Ward, London, George Allen, 1912).

[6] See Parsons, Talcott, *The Structure of Social Action* (1937) (The Free Press
of Glencoe, New York,1964), 43–51; also, importantly, n. 5 *supra* and 9 *infra*.

[7] See Durkheim, Emile, *The Rules of Sociological Method* (8th edn. by G.E.G.
Catlin (ed.), S.A. Solovay, and J.H. Mueller (trans.), The Free Press, Illinois,
1958). In the author's preface at pp. lvi–lvii he says:

> Because beliefs and practices . . . come to us from without, it does not follow
> that we receive them passively or without modification. In reflecting on

They need not be imagined to be completely successful in guaranteeing the compliant behaviour of all individuals in accordance with their implicit goals, but, from the point of view of explanation in social science and as a plausible observation, they are immensely powerful determinants of the general flow of activity.

These conceptualisations form our basic ontology. That they appear unavoidable is to say that it is impossible, for the purposes of social science, to conceive of our subject matter without these normative relations. Thus, we find ourselves on the brink of announcing that the concept of society implies or presupposes the concept of structured normative relations or, in other words, a normative system. To speak of society, therefore, is necessarily to speak of a normative structure, and it will be no surprise to those familiar with the central texts of sociological jurisprudence and basic legal anthropology[8] that this conception of societal fundamentals doubles amazingly well as a concept of law. Unger says[9]:

> In the broadest sense, law is simply any recurring mode of interaction among individuals and groups, together with more or less explicit acknowledgement by these groups and individuals that such patterns of interaction produce reciprocal expectations of conduct that ought to be satisfied.

> collective institutions and assimilating them for our selves, we individualize them and impart to them more or less personal characteristics. . . . It is for this reason that each one of us creates, in a measure, his own morality, religion and mode of life. There is no conformity to social convention that does not comprise an entire range of individual shades. It is nonetheless true that this field of variations is a limited one. It verges on nonexistence or is very restricted in that circle of religious and moral affairs where deviation easily becomes crime. It is wider in all that concerns economic life. But sooner or later, even in the latter instance, one encounters the limit that cannot be crossed.

[8] *Cf.* e.g. Llewellyn, K., 'The Normative, the Legal and the Law Jobs; The Problem of Juristic Method' (1940) 49 *Yale LJ* 1373; Roberts, Simon, *Order and Dispute* (Pelican Books, Harmondsworth,1979); also Twining, William, *Karl Llewellyn and the Realist Movement* (Weidenfeld and Nicolson, London, 1985), esp. 175ff.

[9] Unger, Roberto M., *Law in Modern Society* (Free Press, New York, 1976), 53.

We are close to making an important connection here between law (as an object of inquiry) and social theory, in that, at its most basic, law must be regarded as, at least, the attempt to subject human conduct to some form of normative predictability. Thus law as a discrete institution, like society as a whole, is conceived as a systematic normative phenomenon. This characterisation, which begs no important questions about the concept of law, is simply the thinnest conception of law which is possible for the purposes of argument *about* the concept of law. But it runs the risk of making too close a connection. For there is an apparent impasse in the attempt to appropriate the concept of law with the methodological tools of sociological theory. That is, the approach to understanding law as an aspect of regulation from a sociological perspective leads us to the point where we must acknowledge that all societies conceived as wholes, and all societal institutions conceived as parts of the whole, must be understood as regulatory systems. Thus we must ask whether or not all such systems and sub-systems of regulation are to be designated legal, or, on the other hand, is there some special set of characteristics which render one regulatory system or sub system legal, whilst another is designated non-legal or pre-legal? Of course, one can stipulate whatever criterion of demarcation one wishes, but let us note at this point that merely stipulating certain features of a regulatory system as those features which are constitutive of the legal, without some essential or logically compelling justification—i.e. following what might be termed a conventionalist approach to the concept of law—is not in the least helpful other than to settle the contingently approved usage of a word. Further we can note that selecting contingent procedural, professional or technological features of a normative system in this way, whilst (as we noted in Chapter 1 *supra*), this might be heuristically useful in isolating types of social order for various classificatory purposes, cannot hope to deliver a theory of *obligation*.

This is important because although we want to see law as an integral part of the regulatory structure of society, we do not want to say that all regulation is law, or that law is society. We

need only reflect that, just as in political theory, a notion of political institutions bereft of a theory of political obligation is worth-
less in that it does not provide a distinction between *autoritas*
and *potestas*, so too is a concept of law which contains no criterion of practical reason for compliance which might allow us
meaningfully to distinguish the types of obligation imposed by,
for example, the demands of an armed robber, the requirements
of basic economic co-operation in the tribe, or the injunctions of
what is held to be a developed legal system. The attempt to present a theory of obligation in this way leads, of course, to a consideration of why an individual or group ought rationally to
comply with certain norms. This seems to lead straight to the
central concerns of moral philosophy and, for the moment at
least, it is probably advisable to defer attention to these issues.

Given the obvious difficulties in producing a convincing theory of obligation for the purposes of legal or political theory,
might it not be that we are on firmer, if less ambitious, grounds
in confining our efforts to the more general aims of social theory. Can sociology, as distinct from legal theory, political theory
or sociological jurisprudence, pass over the issue of demarcating
the legal from the non-legal, and the perhaps embarrassing
issues of justification of norms and thus of obligations to obey
them? After all, there seems to be no obvious reason why a sociological understanding of the nature of society must first
respond to the peculiar preoccupations of jurisprudence. But
simply from the point of view of explanation in social science it
seems that we must meet issues of value head-on. Let us consider precisely why it is that the attempt to complete the
explanatory scheme leads us, perhaps unintentionally, into the
realms of legal, political, and moral judgement.

Rethinking the Concept of 'Function'

We are tugged in this direction because of the requirement to
construct a scheme of explanation which allows us to make
sense of the elements of the social system or structure. Here we
arrive at an important point in the argument; for, as Durkheim

suggested and Parsons and Merton later discussed in detail, the notion of system or *structure* leads inexorably to the adoption of the explanatory device of system *function*.[10] That this notion should intrude into all or the vast majority of sociological discussion is hardly surprising, given the ubiquity of forms of functionalist explanation 'the central orientations' of which, quite simply, are 'expressed in the practice of interpreting data by establishing their consequences for larger structures in which they are implicated'.[11]

This simple point is crucially important. When, in 1949, Kingsley Davis asserted that 'all sociology is functionalist sociology', this was perhaps misinterpreted as a lack of awareness on his part of the rise of counter-currents in 'actionist', Marxist and Weberian inspired perspectives. But the point is (and Davies' and Merton's point might have been) that, notwithstanding different schools and nomenclatures, our explanatory options are severely limited in respect of social and historical phenomena if we are to search beyond biology and the conscious intentions of socially located individuals.[12] But proprietary brands of struc-

[10] See Merton, Robert K., *Social Theory and Social Structure* (Free Press, New York, 1957). *Cf.* Giddens, A., 'Functionalism: Apres la lutte' in his *Studies in Social and Political Theory* (Hutchinson,1979) esp. 96, 97. The kind of analysis of the logic of functionalist explanation contained in this piece is important in this context. There is no great difficulty in understanding a functional model of anything—the problem lies with conscious, purposive individuals who are held to be component parts of a functional system and yet capable of understanding the whole from a perspective which appears logically to transcend the whole. See also Giddens, Anthony, *Durkheim* (Fontana, 1978), chaps. 1 and 2; and Durkheim, n. 5 *supra*.

[11] Merton, n. 10 *supra*, 46, 47.

[12] Interactionist (sometimes phenomenological or ethnomethodological) approaches to social science emphasise the processes by which meaning is created by individuals in their various situations and experiences. This is an important area of sociological literature, but most of the significant contributions to this field rely on some idea of a normative background or existing context to the production of meaning. In so far as this determines or attenuates individual interpretations of experience or relationships it alludes, we argue, to a social structure or a system, and thus some explanation of the nature of this structure. Once the concept of structure is adopted as an ontological tenet, we cannot then logically avoid the notion of function. This is what *we* would mean if we were to

tural-functionalism were indeed under attack in the 1950s—a period which ironically might be considered as hegemonic for functionalist sociology—and in Merton's invaluable *Social Theory and Social Structure*[13] he responds, in chapter 1, to a host of interpretations of the alleged theoretical postulates of functionalist methodology. Most ideological charges against functionalism can be traced to the characterisation of these postulates as comprising the notions of (i) the functional *unity* of society (ii) the *universality* of function, and (iii) the *indispensability* of function. Where (i) is interpreted to imply the inevitable tendency to *harmony* in a system; where (ii) follows Malinowski's view that, '[t]he functional view of culture *insists* therefore upon the principle that in *every type of civilization, every custom, material object, idea and belief fulfils some vital function* . . .; and where (iii) equates to the assertion that certain cultural or social forms are regarded as indispensable and irreplaceable structures; then, as Merton says, this gives rise to all manner of difficulties. Not least is the tendency to a conservative bias in purportedly disinterested sociological analysis. Merton, however, is highly critical of these assumptions within and *about* functionalist explanation, and we are inclined to endorse his views in this regard. But our aim is not to promote or rehabilitate an ideologically sanitised form of functionalism; rather we are suggesting that cruder forms of it persist in influential examples of legal theory. Thus we wish to make some general observations on the 'functionalism' of examples of *legal theory* in so far as their allusions to social order in relation to 'background' or 'social' necessity implicitly incorporate the problematic postulates noted immediately above.

announce that all sociology is functionalist. See, importantly, Merton, Robert K., *Social Theory and Social Structure* (Free Press, New York, 1957), chap. 1; also see the discussion in Beyleveld and Wiles (n. 3 *supra*). For an informative introductory discussion on the rise of brands of functionalism see Bilton *et al.*, *Introductory Sociology* (2nd edn., Macmillan, London, 1987), 568ff.

[13] Merton (n. 10 *supra*), 25ff.

Durkheim, Weber and Marx?

We have made a case for the indispensability of the notion of social structure in any comprehensive approach to the characterisation and explanation of processes of social action. It is the idea of structure alone which leads us to the concept of 'function', and, we maintain, the need for the description of functional units (broadly, institutions) in ideal-typical terms. We need only draw Marx into the equation and we have the prospect of integrating what are commonly held to be the representative factions of the great sociological divide. But the divide is mythical and such a synthesis is no great discovery: Merton's chapter referred to above is enough to dispel reservations to the contrary; and he and Lipset and Young offer a plethora of insights and examples of functional explanation in a range of social and political theory. Lipset, for example, draws our attention to Marx and Toqueville in this regard. He says[14]:

> The difference between the approaches of Toqueville and Marx did not necessarily result in contradictory analyses of the functions of various social institutions, although it did make for a very different *evaluation* of the same processes and mechanism. Marx's statement that religion is the 'opiate of the masses' is a recognition of its integrative function. Toqueville also recognised the 'opiative' function of religion: 'Religion, then, is simply another form of hope . . .' To Marx religion was a source of delusion for the lower strata, a mechanism to adjust them to their lot in life and to prevent them from recognizing their *true class interests* [our emphasis].

Merton, similarly, notes that[15]:

> It is in the evaluation of [the] functions of religion, rather than in the logic of analysis, then, that the functionalists and the Marxists part company. And it is the *evaluations* which permit the pouring of ideological content into the bottles of *functionalism* [original emphasis].

[14] Lipset, Seymour M., 'Political Sociology' in Merton, Robert. K. (ed.), *Sociology Today* (Basic Books Inc., New York, 1960), 81–114, at 88.

[15] Merton (n. 9 *supra*), 45.

Let us note two things in respect of these quotations above. First, and inevitably, we are directed not to the problem of the *form* of explanation, but of its substance: *viz.*, the *evaluation* of function in terms of 'real' or 'true' interests. Secondly, it appears that some notion of real or true interests is required as a framework of orientation *prior* to instituting a functionalist investigation of any social system. Merton is right then to deflect criticism of functional explanation *per se* as being 'conservative'—it might just as easily appear as revolutionary. But a formal problem does remain between these extremes. Gunnar Myrdal might have benefited from a reading of Merton's critique of the more extravagant postulates of functionalism, but he highlights a general concern for the status of objectivity of social theory in general when he says[16]:

> if a thing has a 'function' it is good or at least essential. The term 'function' can have a meaning only in terms of an assumed *purpose*; if that purpose is left undefined or implied to be the 'interest of society' which is not further defined, a considerable leeway for arbitrariness in practical implication is allowed but the main direction is given: a *description of social institutions in terms of their functions must lead to a conservative teleology.*

Merton, in rejecting this observation, rightly points to Myrdal's assumption of the necessary employment of the postulates of functional *unity* and functional *indispensability*. We might also note in respect of functional goods that functionalism in general is quite aware of the notion of *dys*function. But of Myrdal's suggestion that the notion of function can only have meaning 'in terms of an assumed *purpose*', Merton remarks that this is 'not only gratuitous, but false'.[17] We need not be drawn into Myrdal's error in respect of the assumption of exclusively conservative tendencies within functionalist explanation; but the issue of system, function and purpose does demand our attention. Primarily, this is because the idea of system or structure

---

[16] Myrdal, Gunnar, *An American Dilemma* (Harper and Brothers, New York, 1944), ii, 1056; quoted in Merton. (n. 10 *supra*), 37.

[17] Merton (n 10 *supra*), 37, n. 35.

does, as Myrdal notes, inevitably prompt questions about the purpose of the *whole*. We might benefit from a brief but cautious recap of the issues here which can be categorised under four related heads and referred to as follows:

(i) 'the teleological fallacy';
(ii) the problem of ideology;
(iii) the problem of the concept of 'system equilibrium' (or social order);
(iv) the problem of the whole; that is, the issue of whether making sense of the normative institutional relations in society involves attributing some conception of purposive rationality to the social whole. This is to claim that the social system, the whole which we call 'society', has a purpose, and this is very different from saying that all individuals have purposes, or that particular institutions in society have functions in terms of the whole system.

The teleological fallacy, in general, can be explained as the tendency to attempt to account for the existence of a thing by inventing or even demonstrating some purpose (or function) of the object in question. This, in many cases, is scientifically unsound reasoning in that, first, it involves the initial assumption that if an object exists it must exist for a particular purpose and, secondly, that if the purpose can be gleaned, the statement of the purpose (or function) of the object can then be announced as the *cause* of the existence of the object. This knowledge is then held to yield an insight into the essential nature of the object. All manner of fantasies can be 'justified' by the ingenious application of this method, and there has been a longstanding debate about the propriety of this form of reasoning since Aristotle.[18]

This general disquiet has been levelled at versions of functionalist social theory and, we suggest, is mistaken, in so far as it rules out the validity of teleological reasoning *per se*. It is not,

[18] See e.g., Barnes, Jonathan, *Aristotle* (Oxford University Press, Oxford, 1982), 51–7.

as Merton points out, a required postulate of functional explanation. However, some notion of purpose is vitally relevant
when presented as what we have referred to in (ii) as the problem of *ideology*. Thus we have two points to consider. First, let
us simply note that our earlier argument for the indispensability
of the ideal-type is an argument which, in short, holds that purposive (practical) phenomena must be apprehended as such:
teleological explanation is appropriate to objects assumed to be
possessed of a *telos*. Secondly, however, the opportunities and
tendencies to abuse this methodological form have proved irresistible in that few theoretical exercises are less taxing or more
gratifying than the pastime of inventing internally consistent and
all-embracing teleological networks. This not only ensnares the
well-meaning into delusions of truth, it presents *carte blanche* to
ideologues who, employing arbitrary notions of historical ends
or tendencies, might wish to weave the strands of sectional interest into the theoretical presentation of the structure of social or
natural reality. Thus, the problem of ideology is acute and, we
think, in this form relates more specifically to (iii) the problem
of the concept of equilibrium and (iv) the problem of 'the
whole'. In relation to the issue of ideology, these constitute one
and the same problem. Let us consider for a moment Myrdal's
point in relation to a general (more or less Durkheimian) scheme
of functional explanation.

Briefly, Durkheimian social theory and the later derivative
forms of 'structural functionalism'[19] conceive of society as an
organic whole. In Durkheim's work we see a direct application of
the analogy of the animal organism to the problem of constructing a basic ontology of the social system. In order to maintain
itself as an integral whole through time, certain aspects of system
maintenance must be carried out. Major parts of the whole in
combination with each other are understood as performing vital
system functions which maintain the whole in equilibrium. For
example, when we ask why institutions such as the family or religion persist as major features of social organisation, we might be

[19] See, e.g., Bilton *et al. Introductory Sociology* (2nd Edn., Macmillan Press,
Basingstoke, 1987), 556–71.

told that they perform socialising and stabilising functions: they produce the cement which binds the whole together. But, first, this assumes that we can identify stability or order, for if we could not, we could not identify a functional unit operating in terms of a stabilising *process*. In short, first, identifying system stability as a *consequence* of some *internal* dynamic leads us to infer, secondly, that it is the result of a causal *process*, and, thirdly, invites us to investigate and identify the sub-system and analyse the nature of its causal interrelations within the total system. This directly raises the question of how we characterise social order—a notion which admits of a great range of moral, economic and aesthetic interpretation, and in itself is enough to render the concept of function ideologically 'wild' and thus theoretically unstable.

Further problems lie with the issue of the *purpose* or function of the *whole*—the system *itself*. That this issue is not discussed or immediately apparent is not to say that no conception of purpose is in operation in this type of explanation. Merton regards this objection as 'gratuitous', but, we suggest, from the point of view of conscious inhabitants of a social system, questions about the purpose of the whole cannot be avoided—and are, perhaps, always implicit in social theory. Despite an antipathy to detailed discussion of this issue, there is a revelation in Durkheim of the existence of the hidden assumption of the mysterious purpose of the social whole. Durkheim, in seeking to explain the phenomenon of suicide in purely structural terms was, eventually, forced to account for the nature of the causal nexus which converts a macro system-state (i.e. a rate of integration) into a rate of suicide. Alex Inkeles explains[20]:

> To the question of how the origin of suicide could lie in the degree of integration of a social structure, he [Durkheim] replied by referring to man's 'psychological constitution' which, he said, 'needs an object transcending it'. This object is lacking in the weakly integrat-

---

[20] Inkeles, Alex, in Merton, Robert K., *Sociology Today* (Basic Books Inc., New York, 1960), 252, quoting from Durkheim's *Suicide* (Spaulding, J.A. and Simpson, G. (trans.), New York, Free Press, 1951).

ed society, and consequently 'the individual, having too keen a feeling for himself and his own value . . . wishes to be his own only goal, and as such an objective cannot satisfy him, drags out languidly an existence which henceforth seems meaningless to him.'

Now this is a very troublesome admission for any form of functionalist theory. It is tantamount to asserting that the purpose of the social whole is to constitute a necessary focal point for the human psyche, a focal point without which the individual personality disintegrates into literally terminal *ennui*. Thus, logically, the maintenance of the whole in some minimum condition of integrity is seen to be a precondition of the well-being of all individuals regardless of their particular purposes. We cannot avoid pursuing this issue.

When we talk of a system or a structure, or, if we add the dimension of development through time, a process, we presuppose the existence of understandable relations between parts and the whole. This means ordered relations which admit of some possibility of explanation, as opposed to a chaotic jumble of phenomena. To illustrate the point we can note that a scrap heap can be seen as an object 'composed' of metal parts, and so can the engine of an Aston Martin. But the relations between the 'parts' of the scrap heap and the nature of any particular 'part' of the heap cannot be explained in terms of function. However, because an object like a sophisticated engine is almost intuitively and immediately conceived as a systemic whole with a particular purpose (that of providing rotary motion for the purposes of yet other discrete systems) we are furnished with a complete and comprehensive system of explanation pertaining to each and every part and each and every relationship between these parts. But here the idea of the whole—the engine—is conceptually different from the intuitive idea we posses of the social whole: for we do not regard the engine as an *environment* which determines (to some extent) the behaviour of the parts or facilitates their continued existence. Rather we simply see the engine as a functional *product* of the configured properties of the parts. The difference is quite considerable, in that speaking of the continued existence of the social whole as the explanation of the functions of the parts is analogous to saying that the purpose of an automobile engine—its very *raison d'être*—is to provide a rational justification for the existence of all the relations between the parts: oil pump, injectors, plugs, distributor, filters, valves and so on and so forth down to the last thread on the last bolt. In the example at hand, this is theoretically problematic for two reasons: (a) it implicitly denies the plain truth that the whole system (the complete engine) does, in fact, have a further purpose, that of supplying the power for rotary motion to other systems, and (b) because, in appealing to the integrity of the whole as our frame of orientation for an inquiry into the nature of the parts, this denial of continuing purpose serves to arrest and reverse the logical direction of explanation, effectively turning it in on itself. We must then be careful in choosing, or assuming, a logical direction of functional explanation and orientation. But which explanatory path should we follow? Parsons, in differentiating the ideas of structure, system and process, says[21];

> Thus, to make it as clear as possible, the concept 'function' unlike that of structure and of process, is not a rubric in terms of which an immediately empirical description of a set of features of a living system can be stated. . . . Its reference is to the formulation of sets of conditions governing the states of living systems as 'going concerns' in relation to their environments. These conditions concern the stability and/or instability, the survival and/or probable extinction, and not least, the temporal duration of such systems.
>
> . . . The concept 'function', then . . . concerns, above all, the consequences of the existence and nature of certain empirically describable structures and processes in such systems. Included, of course, are considerations relevant to the conditions under which the structures and processes of reference can arise, or the probabilities that they will in fact develop, or persist.

Let us try to be even clearer. Our central point has been that, given the idea of social *structure*, some type of functional explanation is unavoidable in social science. As we have seen, this is the *evaluation* of the function of certain *institutional processes* in

---

[21] Parsons (n. 5 *supra*), 70.

terms of, as Parsons says, *consequences*. But consequences for what: the total system, or the large-scale yet still component or sub- 'structures and processes of reference', or perhaps, and quite plausibly, individual 'personality systems'—i.e. you and me? The larger the 'structures and processes of reference' turn out to be, the nearer to questions about 'consequences' for the whole we get. In short, we think that the issue of ideology or of *purpose* raised and rebuffed in various forms for and against functionalist explanation must inevitably boil down to the question of the evaluation of consequences of system stability in terms of some conception of human interest.

This becomes clear the harder we press the issue of normative rationality in general, and legality and legal obligation in particular. Let us assume we have a scheme of functional explanation where rational purpose is explicitly imputed to the whole, the implicit assumption, therefore, is that the maintenance of the social whole is intrinsically rational—an *end in itself*—for the maintenance of its integrity appeals to no further conditioning purpose. The normative arrangements (institutions, values, 'laws') which are then alleged to contribute to the maintenance of the whole are thus functionally 'explained'. This 'reversed' scheme of explanation is very different, however, from the suggestion that the purpose of sustaining the orderly integrity of the social whole is to provide the type of environment which, in, say, Hobbes' or Rousseau's account of state and society, is held to be a precondition of the successful pursuit of various *individual* purposes.[22] Let us consider the implications of the differences in explanation in respect of the issue of compliance or obligation with institutional norms.

[22] Hobbes is clear: orderly social relations are prudentially necessary for all individual persons, not only for their mortal security but for the possibility of a genuinely human existence and the pursuit of Christ's Kingdom on Earth. Rousseau too is explicit about the necessity of orderly social relations—the very idea of society—as a means to the individual's pursuit of civilised freedom and the higher good. See Hobbes, Thomas, *Leviathan* (C.B. McPherson (ed.), London, Pelican, 1968), *Introduction*, 39–42; Rouseau, J.J., *The Social Contract and Discourses* (London, Dent, Everyman's Library, 1983), *Introduction* by G.D.H. Cole.

71

To suggest that the maintenance of the social whole is a categorically rational *end*, and that institutions are, jointly and severally, a necessary *means* to this end, is to hold that a rational person would comply with the norms intrinsic to these institutions. The converse implication, that non-compliance is irrational, is equally obvious. But this approach to sociological theory does not appear to consider the possibility of a clash between, on the one hand, the requirements of system maintenance and, on the other, the disparate variety of individual purposes.

The second option for explanation, namely, the assumption that the maintenance of the whole is a *conditional end*, i.e. is a necessary condition of the successful pursuit of purposes held as goals by *individual* persons or groups, does take account of this possibility, but implies that any individual or group with purposes would have to regard the maintenance of the whole as rational *whatever* his or her purposes. In other words, maintenance of the social whole is such a fundamental condition that, in effect, it again must be perceived as categorically rational, although now for more complex and 'dispositional' prudential reasons.[23] From the perspective of individuals within this system, to accept either version of this functional explanation implies acceptance of the practical imperatives (many of which are moral imperatives—i.e. both categorical and 'other-regarding' imperatives) embodied in the normative arrangements of our system. In other words, there is, in a sense, a moral, or at least a prescriptive, sub-text to what is presented as a 'positivistic' (a non-judgemental, non-evaluative, 'scientific') explanation of the nature of the social structure.

It is no revelation to announce that some structural-functionalist conceptions of, for example, the family or religion or, perhaps most notoriously, gender roles and social stratification, have been denounced as 'ideological' or 'value-laden'. This is quite true in the sense that they disingenuously purport to be value-neutral conceptions when they are in fact hefty endorse-

[23] See our discussion in Chap. 6 *infra* of Alan Gewirth's conception of the necessary dispositional goods of agency.

ments of particular forms of moral, social and sexual organisation which bolster fairly obvious interest perspectives. This is
particularly true of aspects of the *status quo* which suit the rich,
the male and the politically powerful. But if we look at precisely
why these charges of moral or ideological impartiality have been
levelled at functionalist explanations we might begin to understand that all forms of sociological explanation—including direct
Marxist assaults on functionalism—are, in an important sense
both functionalist *and* value-laden or morally or ideologically par-
tial. Let us, then, move to the precise point of these rather pro-
tracted preparatory discussions in the attempt to illustrate these
tendencies in aspects of legal theory which appear to rely straightforwardly on unreconstructed functionalist assumptions.

Functionalist Jurisprudence?

There is little doubt that Karl Llewellyn's 'Law Jobs' theory
appears to be remarkably similar to the Durkheimian/Parsonian
conception of explanation. Llewellyn, famously, offers a concept
of law as that complex of regulatory and co-ordinatory tasks (the
law jobs) which any human group of any size must perform successfully if that group is to remain integral as a group. Rightly,
he says that there are certain aspects of dispute resolution,
decision-making and policy formulation which must be performed if a society or, microcosmically, a social sub-group is to
remain integral.[24] This is very close to what Merton, above, calls
the postulate of *indispensability*, wherein certain structural forms
are held to be essential to the maintenance of the whole. If we
are not pressed to accept further specification of the content of
these forms this claim seems to be an unavoidable *a priori*
assumption for the purposes of any explanatory scheme of social
theory. At this general level, then, this is a necessary truth which
is neither illegitimate nor tautologous (in the sense of viciously
circular, or vacuously stipulative). But we must note that here in
Llewellyn we again encounter some ambiguity about the status

[24] See note 25 *infra*.

of the related presupposition that the maintenance of the social whole is the rational end or goal of the system of inter-related sub-tasks or 'law jobs', regardless of the specific purposes of the group or of the individuals which comprise it.

The law jobs, as Llewellyn presents them, appear to subsume all regulatory phenomena. However, we suggested earlier that specifically *legal*, as distinct from general, social theory needs to move towards a differentiation within the general category of regulatory phenomena, or fail to demarcate the legal from the social. In Llewellyn, the goal of regulation in general is the maintenance of the social whole, but law is not simply equated with regulation, nor is it the source of order in the whole. For Llewellyn, 'education', or the complex processes of the transmission of information, ways of seeing, encouragement and discouragement through the family, teachers and social intercourse, provides this stabilising force. Rather, law, for Llewellyn, is the mechanism through which the right amount and the right type of order is produced—and too much unsubtle order is, according to Llewellyn, stifling and a hindrance to the creative or innovative spirit. Law, he held, lubricates the normative order and creates the required amount of 'free play'.[25] Where there is 'free play' there will be disputes, hence the central importance of dispute resolution and the idea of allocation of authoritative 'say'. Llewellyn is straying here from the straightness and narrowness of the path of an acceptable version of the *indispensability* postulate in an effort to articulate his undoubtedly valuable insights into the complex mechanisms of fine-tuning the process of societal regulation. But, clearly, he does not escape (nor needs to) from broadly functionalist premises. In other words, law is conceived as that subset of normative phenomena which directly

[25] See Llewellyn, Karl, *The Bramble Bush* esp. the chapter, 'Law and Civilisation' (New York, Oceana Publications, 1930). Here Llewellyn's remarks are similar to Durkheim's notions of the innovative and progressive forces of change brought about by dispute and dissent. Durkheim goes so far as to say that crime is a functionally stabilising and functionally progressive source of new ideas. Cf. Heathcote, F., 'Social Disorganisation Theories' in *Crime and Society* (London, RKP, 1981), 346ff.

and crucially contributes to shaping the *mode* of stability of the social whole. Law, it seems, attenuates the social system in a manner which can in some way be regarded as 'rational' or 'suitable' or 'viable' in terms of, perhaps, the system's own (mysterious) or, more likely, the individuals' largely unspecified[26] purposes.

Here, then, if we have been fair to Karl Llewellyn, we have an analogy with versions of Durkheimian and later functionalist social theory. For if the maintenance of the whole is a categorically rational goal,[27] and the law jobs are, among other things, necessary means to this end, then, speaking formally and in the sense that we have ascribed this consequence to functionalism in general, compliance with the imperatives of the law or the law jobs must be held to be rational. The collateral, and perhaps unsuccessful, attempt to differentiate the legal from the non-legal in this general context does not alter the functionalist logic: Twining says of Llewellyn[28]:

> By maintaining that law was only one of the institutions which perform the law-jobs in society, he was committed to accepting some distinction, albeit not a rigid one, between it and other institutions. In both 'The Normative, The Legal and The Law Jobs' and in *Law in Our Society* he went very near to providing a definition by suggesting four characteristics which, when combined, serve to differentiate 'legal' from other institutions: specialized personnel or procedures recognized as carrying the stamp of authority of the whole, supremacy within the group, effectiveness and regularity. This aspect of Llewellyn's elucidation of 'law' adds little that is new and it has been improved upon by other jurists, notably Professor Hart.

Llewellyn, then, gives us a concept of law as a system of norms the purpose of which is to maintain the social whole. But,

---

[26] We say 'largely unspecified', because there is, of course, clearly implied a reference to the need for or desirability of an atmosphere in which 'creativity' and 'innovation' might flourish.

[27] Effectively to be regarded as an *end in itself* regardless of anyone's particular wants or purposes.

[28] Twining, William, *Karl Llewellyn and the Realist Movement* (Wiedenfeld and Nicolson, London, 1985), 179.

as we have previously had occasion to note, this is what classical conceptions of *society itself* amount to. For social theorists who adopt this approach to explanation this has the irksome consequence of attracting the objection that either the system is an *end in itself*, or there is a hidden agenda of individual interests which require the maintenance of the system. For legal theorists it is worse, they are vulnerable to this criticism *and* find themselves engaged in a desperate attempt to find a distinguishing criterion for that sub-set of norms which they seek to characterise as 'legal'. Llewellyn, unconvincingly, opts for organisational features of the phenomenon. Hart, somewhat more ingeniously, but, as we hope to show, with much the same methodological assumptions, faces the same problem.

Herbert Hart, of course, has achieved an influential position in modern jurisprudence through his widely discussed work, *The Concept of Law*. Here he offers a critique of Austin and Bentham's 'command theory' of law and suggests we adopt a 'fresh start' from a broadly sociological point of view. He offers a legal positivist (non-moral) conception of law as an institutional response to the problems of human social existence through an explication of the prerequisites of social stability. He attempts to differentiate simple regulatory (pre-legal) systems from what he regards as genuinely legal systems by reference to the notion of the 'unity of primary and secondary rules'—especially the idea of a 'rule of recognition'.[29] He further, and famously, distinguishes law from morals. His suggestion is that the organisational complexity and 'efficiency' of advanced normative (legal) systems remedy the defects of pre-legal arrangements. Together with his (perhaps Lockean) account of notions of natural and irreducible forbearances universally required for social life to succeed (which he terms 'the minimum content of natural law'[30]), and with constant allusions to what in our introductory chapter we referred to as the 'background of social necessity', his claim is to have provided a theory of obligation

[29] See Hart, H.L.A., *The Concept of Law* (2nd edn., Clarendon Press, Oxford, 1994), chap. VI.

[30] *Ibid.*, 189–95.

which is distinguished both from 'obligation' under threat and obligation based on moral judgement. But Hart talks about the goal of humanity as survival, the 'minimum content' of natural law, prerequisites for survival, 'viable' societies, and the need to institutionalise promising and obligations in order that authority (for government) may be established. These arrangements, he says, need not be based on universal principles of morality, nor, he observes, have they been. He adverts to the 'painful facts of human history' which show us that 'though a society to be viable must offer *some* of its members a system of mutual forbearances, it need not, unfortunately, offer them to all'.[31] Hart goes on to talk about 'authority' in this presumably 'viable' society which[32]:

> may be used to subdue and maintain, in a position of permanent inferiority, a subject group whose size, relatively to the master group, may be large or small, depending on the means of coercion, solidarity and discipline available to the latter, and the helplessness or inability to organize of the former. For those thus oppressed there may be nothing in the system to command their loyalty but only things to fear. They are its victims, not its beneficiaries.

This is illuminating. A *descriptive* or positivistic account of legal obligation relying on the alleged necessity of 'social order' must, ultimately, defend the beneficiaries as against the victims, or abandon the notion of 'viable' order as the basis for the account of obligation. This is a clear demonstration of the potential ideological content of the idea of 'order', 'equilibrium', 'stasis', 'social necessity', 'system viability' and so on, which is called upon to do so much *explanatory* work in *all* forms of functionalist explanation, and is assumed to do so much *justificatory* work in purportedly descriptive accounts of law and the nature of legal obligation.

In the light of these reflections on social theory in general, and on Hart and Llewellyn in particular, let us make a few points which illustrate our initial remarks about the integral importance of the concept of law for social theory. By making clear just what

[31] *Ibid.*, 196.
[32] *Ibid.*, 197.

is entailed by the attempt to differentiate basic forms of social regulation, in the sense of contingently effective coercion, from rationally grounded forms of regulation in the form of law, we may be able to provide the basis of an understanding of what it would mean to adopt a genuinely interdisciplinary conception of law and social theory.

A Fresh Start?

First, let us be clear that to speak of society in methodological terms is to speak from the perspective of a cognitive interest within it. We thus conceptualise society as a total system constituting a relatively stable and enduring environment of structured normative arrangements. Behaviour-shaping order is expressed at various levels within this total system. To speak of law is to have in mind something very similar existing *within* the total system yet fundamentally, and functionally, often appearing indistinguishable from it. We should not be surprised, then, if problematic consequences of analysis stemming from the attempt to conceptualise *society* similarly accrue to legal theory sociologically conceived. That is, objections to ideological bias and anxieties about implicit conceptions of *system-purpose* in social theory are actually objections to the tacit *legitimation* of institutional norms in the purported attempt merely to *explain* them. In legal theory this strategy surfaces in three stages in the attempt to *differentiate the legal* from the generally regulatory structure of society. Stage (i) involves the implicit assumption of the postulate of *indispensability* of certain functional forms of regulation and co-ordination. Stage (ii) sees the move from this assumption to the attempt to (a) 'recognise' or attach identificatory characteristics to forms of regulation *in terms of non-practical criteria* (such as procedural or professional styles of organisation or promulgation) (b) differentiate these forms from 'custom', and (c) designate as 'legal' (meaning 'legitimately enforceable') the normative *content* of these allegedly indispensable forms of regulation. Stage (iii) seeks to present the idea of legal obligation as arising from the fusion of the organisational,

78

procedural or 'official' enforcement features of certain norms—attributes which, in themselves, are irrelevant to the issue of *legitimate* practical reason for compliance—with the *imperative* implicit in the postulate of *indispensability* initially assumed in stage (i).[33] This is doubly disingenuous. First, whilst we might all agree that co-ordinatory and regulatory *forms* such as policy-making, dispute-resolution or the allocation of an authoritative 'say' might be indispensable to the maintenance of a social system, *and* agree that these features of it were consonant with all individual interests, there is a chasm between this proposition and agreement on suitable conceptions of how these forms might be expressed in institutional *substance*. Secondly, and related to the first, no amount of organisational complexity, codification, professionalisation or procedural pedigree[34] attached to a norm can, by themselves, provide a rational justification of general applicability for compliance with it and, hence, genuinely be said to induce an obligation.[35]

This problematic symmetry between social theory and legal theory is to be expected in the light of the shared conception of society as a functional system of ordered normative relations, and the often implicit imputation of rationality to the whole. To speak of the maintenance of this order is to introduce some notion of a systemic purpose through which it is possible to explain the functional dynamics of normative elements of the structure. This much seems to be unavoidable in the construction of a basic ontology for social science. But we have seen how this attempt to ground the existence of normative institutions in rationality—that is, *explain* them—is equivalent to claiming that

[33] That is, the hidden implication that the maintenance of the social whole is prudentially relevant to the interests of all groups and individuals, thus, as a matter of practical reason, one *ought* to comply with institutional processes seen as *indispensable* means to the maintenance of the whole.

[34] This is to assume, in this context, that 'procedure' is a non-moral concept. Genuinely legal procedure, however, arises from moral concerns, as we noted in Chap. 2 *supra* and as we discuss further in Chap. 6 *infra*.

[35] This is not to say that subjective conceptions of what is prudent might contingently coincide with compliance. But, as Hart says, this is no theory of law or legal obligation. See our discussion in Chap. 1 *supra*.

it is rational (i.e. 'one ought . . .') to comply with them. But these justifications of norms implicit in functionalist theory are addressed, in the form of explanations, to the individuals who are part of the social system and significantly constitutive of it. This, of course, is why versions of functionalism which assume the inevitability of harmonious unity are rightly accused of a moral or ideological bias. For the logic of simultaneously explaining the existence of, and justifying compliance with, a norm or set of norms via this conceptual scheme assumes that the desirability of maintaining the integrity of the social whole is consistent with, if not a precondition of, securing interests of all or most individuals located in the system. The real debate starts here, for it is by no means clear why this should be thought to be the case. Where allusions to 'social' or 'functional necessity' occur, we must be alert to the possibility that the assumption of the harmonious coincidence of interests between the social system and all or most individuals is implied. If it is, the logic of obligation is irresistible: one cannot both accept that the goal of maintaining the integrity of the social system is categorically rational and hold that compliance with what is required to achieve this system maintenance is contrary to one's own interests—unless one admits that one's purposes are irrational. It is certainly possible and often enjoyable to pursue purposes which one admits to be irrational, but one must admit that, rationally speaking, it is sometimes, perhaps often, the case that one ought not to pursue ends which one does in fact want to pursue. There is a further drawback to this admission, in that if one accepts that the pursuit of system maintenance is rational, and this involves the prohibition or vigorous discouragement of one's purposes, then one must accept that this prohibition is justified and resistance to it is unjustified. In short, if one accepts that system maintenance is rational, one cannot, whatever one's perceived interests may be, and however much the normative arrangements of the system frustrate one's purposes, rationally mount criticism of these arrangements.

This becomes disturbingly clear if we consider the following: what if, as in Hart's scenario, the maintenance of the normative structure of the social whole benefits (i.e. serves the prudential interests of) only a small minority of the individuals who form part of the social collectivity? If so, then the functionalist approach to explanation of the nature of social institutions, although still coherent, implies that the goal of the maintenance of the social whole is to further the interests of this particular minority. Moreover, because of this, if it holds that the maintenance of the whole is intrinsically desirable, i.e. categorically rational, it follows that the prudential interests of this minority, i.e. the achievement of their purposes, ought categorically to be pursued by others on their behalf—even when these others perceive this to be against their own subjectively defined interests, preferences or desires.

If we shift our perspective and vocabulary, call this minority a 'class', and suggest that, because of some special attribute or capacity, this class is instrumental in preserving the normative arrangements of the system over and against the interests of all other individuals, then we see how a general structuralist account might be immediately inverted ideologically. For this is exactly what Marxists say about functionalist social theory. The moral sub-text to Marxism, therefore, is clear when we see that the message is as follows: the normative arrangements which preserve the stability of the social whole serve the interests of a minority—a dominant class. The interests of the minority (the ruling class) are antithetical to the interests of all other individuals (the subject class). If it is rational to act in one's own interest then all individuals belonging to this subject class ought not to comply with the imperatives implicit or explicit in the normative institutional framework of the social whole—in fact they ought to abolish them and supplant them with institutions which would produce a system which served their own interests. The scheme of explanation is exactly the same: bourgeois institutions are explained by reference to their system-functions as perpetuators and protectors of a social whole which operates to preserve bourgeois interests at the expense of proletarian interests. Thus, as we noted earlier, it is exclusively the *conception of human interests* which is at odds with Durkheim's or Parsons' or Toqueville's 'functionalism'.

In terms of a sociologically informed legal theory, if we transfer Llewellyn's conception of law-as-system-maintenance, or Hart's notions of system efficiency, to the hypothetical situation outlined above, then we must admit that the explanations (justifications) of enforcement of legal norms are now implicated in this ugly ideological row. It seems, then, that an undifferentiated conception of 'social order' or of 'system equilibrium', which is not alert to the hidden postulates and assumptions so acutely identified and rejected by Merton and others,[36] might leave itself open to ideological abuse. Such an approach might unwittingly have the consequence of suggesting implicitly that the existing institutional framework serves the interests of all (or perhaps just the majority of) individuals.

Defending the Idea of 'Social Structure'

The notion of the social whole as an organic product of normative institutions, and the imputation of purposive rationality to the whole and the parts based on a conception of order or equilibrium is, we think, indispensable to social science, and thus to a sociologically informed legal science. To conceive of society is to imagine a system which, in an important metaphorical sense, is in some way like this. It is to define society as the product of ordered normative relations and to offer some explanation of the reason for achieving (or striving for) some type of order. Admittedly, this is a requirement of structuralist theory and not a result of empirical observation. The logic of this type of explanation is perfectly sound and can (in fact must) be applied in our attempts to understand mechanical and biological, as well as social, systems. The crucial difference is that in biology and engineering we operate with uncontentious and empirically quantifiable criteria of order and equilibrium in, for instance, the explanation of the pathologies of animal organisms or mechanical systems. Notions of social order on the other hand, presuppose criteria of value in their conceptions of system integrity. A

[36] See nn. 9 and 10 *supra*.

Durkheimian conception of a social system in equilibrium is, on the basis of the same empirical 'data', a system in irreconcilable conflict for Marx. Why the disagreement? Because both theorists operate with different conceptions of human interests. We can make a leap of understanding by noting plainly that the criterion of system equilibrium, or the rational organisation of society, is achieved for each of them when the organisation of the whole is consonant with their respective conceptions of individual human interests.

What, then, are human interests? More precisely, what kind of social organisation would serve the interests of human beings? We are not here simply talking about what human beings might like or say they like. Durkheim and Marx are talking about *real* interests and not subjective preferences. Prudential interests based on personal preferences are contingent and self-defined (unless, of course, they are in some sense necessary for the very possibility of the contemplation of successful agency itself).[37] That is, my prudential interests are served when my chosen purposes—my wants—are fulfilled. But the notion of social order in social and legal theory discussed above, or any conception of social order for that matter, cannot be based upon the notion of prudential interests *simplicit*er. This is because we know that for the maintenance of the equilibrium of the social whole to serve as a valid source of explanation for the parts, the maintenance of the whole must be regarded as either (a) an intrinsic end—a rational *end in itself*, or (b) necessary for the pursuit of individual purposes. If the maintenance of the whole produced the fulfilment of each individual's self-defined purposes, then this would be one way of defining, and understanding, social equilibrium on which everyone could, in a prudential sense, agree. But this is a highly implausible notion of social equilibrium: we need only consider that just one *de facto* disagreement about interests would invalidate this. More importantly, a conception of social order as the situation where everyone would *de facto* agree that their interests were served, i.e. a perpetual 'consensus'

[37] See n. 19 *supra*.

on everything—assumes that it is impossible to be mistaken about one's own interests. In other words, such a theory would assent to the truth of the proposition that the world is organised in my interests if I happen to believe it is, and is not so organised if I do not. This, of course, assuming that system-purpose is consonant with individual interests, would make the equilibrium of the social structure a product of any and every individual's contingent belief states. We could invent a neologism to denote this fantasy—something like: 'projected solipsistic equilibrium'—but whatever we choose to call this state of affairs, suffice it to say that it does not qualify as a credible candidate for incorporation into any coherent social theory. In other words, we cannot hope to work on a conception of social order which equates to a chaotic jumble of unpredictable and unrestricted, self-defined prudential interests. We do not have to solve the problem of grounding a particular criterion of human interests to see that *all* conceptions of social order presuppose *some* criterion of human interests. If we resolve to remain alert to the issue of interests in our dealing with all theory which alludes to the explanation of forms of normative regulation, it seems that we cannot avoid the following conclusions:

(1) In explicitly functionalist social theory and, more importantly, all social theory which utilises the notion of function (and this includes interpretive schemes which employ practical reconstructions or, as we noted, Weberian 'ideal-types' of large scale institutions) explanation based on *tacit* conceptions of human interests are ideological in so far as they implicitly legitimate the institutional structure of a society whilst simultaneously and disingenuously claiming 'positivistic' status or 'value-neutrality'.

(2) In legal theories which attempt to assimilate sociological schemes of explanation that are broadly functionalist, we can note, first, that conceptions of legal phenomena are incomplete in so far as they do not differentiate specifically, and *non-arbitrarily with regard to normative content*, legal phenomena from regulatory phenomena in general. If the differentiation

of the legal from the non-legal requires us at least to view regulation from a perspective of practical reason for compliance and *authoritative* enforcement, then this must raise the issue of legal obligation. Thus *social theory* requires a theory of real or objective human interests if it is to provide an explanatory framework, and *legal theory* requires the same if it is to produce a theory of legal obligation. In other words, moral rationality is fundamentally implicated in the attempt to *apprehend* the social and legal phenomena in question. This should be borne in mind as we move into subsequent chapters.

In the following chapter we respond to the suggestion that the allegedly less problematic notion of democracy might allow us to side-step this apparent methodological impasse and also avoid the ideologically unwelcome consequences of incorporating morality into legal reasoning.

4
Law, Morality or 'The People'?

In this chapter we take the opportunity to examine some contemporary concerns about the relationship between law and the quality of democracy in the modern state. In essence, the problem we examine concerns the suggestion from influential scholars past and present that, as moral reasoning intrudes into judicial and administrative process, the more legality becomes removed from the expressed interests, mechanisms of accountability and constitutional parameters of democratic control. The empirical claim allied to it is that this is increasingly the case in the modern administrative ('welfare' or 'social'[1]) state. The core of the problem, as presented by Ingeborg Maus, suggests an inherent antipathy between a moralised concept of law and the democratic control of legislative and administrative power. She says[2]:

[1] Carl Schmitt speaks of the 'social' state in opposition to the traditional 19th-century notion of the 'neutral' state. These classifications are a matter of degree. Complexity and industrialisation bring with them an increasing plurality of interests, and this is mirrored by increasing governmental responsibility, administration and scope for economic intervention. This interventionist state is contrasted with the 'neutral' state which Schmitt regards as having the primary function of safeguarding society's autonomy against executive power (see n. 8 *infra*). The form of 'social' or 'total' state which Schmitt counterposes to the 19th-century model, however, is modelled on the pathologies of Weimar and thus is not accurately regarded as synonymous with the term which might commonly be used today by public lawyers, i.e. 'the modern administrative state'. See Leydet, Dominique, 'Pluralism and the Crisis of Democracy' (1997) *Canadian Journal of Law and Jurisprudence*, (Vol X, No. 1 January, 1997) 49–77. See also this important edition of *CJLJ* in its entirety—a 10th anniversary edition devoted to analysis and critique of Carl Schmitt's work—edited by David Dyzenhaus.

[2] Maus, Ingeborg, 'The Differentiation Between Law and Morality as a Limitation of Law' in: Aarnio, A., and Tuori, K (eds.), *Law, Morality and*

it is precisely the direct integration of moral principle into the concept of law which breaks down the limits of law and thus removes the limits to state regulation. A consequence of this intrusion of moral principle—and thus of moral reasoning, is that it allows '. . . administrative bodies to impose "constitutional" or "legal" restrictions on individual activities even where no constitutional or legal regulation exists.' The result being an undemocratic and uncontrollable '. . . extension of power held by public administration [including courts] at the cost of the legislature.

The general point she makes, then, is that the capacity for *democratically* approved legislation to restrain the arbitrary exercise of public administrative (i.e. executive, judicial and bureaucratic-discretionary) power will evaporate if departmental officials and judges be allowed to base their exercise of power on *moral* grounds. This leads, it is alleged, to the weakening of the importance of the legislative production of statutory rights, and delivers to the governmental and administrative elite a means to exercise powers that they do not legitimately hold under a democratic constitution: Law, when democratically produced, relates to and protects collective interests and aspirations, but, when *morally* interpreted, it is susceptible to the internal and unaccountable value-perspective of one individual. The not implausible thesis on offer is that the *legitimating* force of the collective is used to empower the state as a legal authority, and that the technique of morally obfuscating, situationising and particularising posited laws allows the democratic and consensual *imprimatur* of the people to be used in ways antithetical to its general interests.[3] There are two central features of this kind of thinking.

Discursive Rationality (Publications of the Departments of Public Law, University of Helsinki, Helsinki, 1988), 141–2. See also developments of this view in her article 'Liberties and Popular Sovereignty: On Jurgen Habermas's Reconstruction of The System of Rights' (1996) 17 *Cardozo Law Review* 825–81.

[3] Maus still seems to employ this view. In her article from 1996 (n. 2 *supra*) she seems to endorse what she calls

'the grounding of democratic freedom in terms of natural law . . ., [which] focuses on ASSYMMETRIES related to the relationship between the

The first is a thorough scepticism in relation to moral principles and moral reasoning. The perception, originally Marxist, of individualised, *a*historical, objectified morality as a form of interest-based ideology and thus a tool for oppression, serves as a starting point for questioning the validity of moral reasoning *per se* and, hence, for rejecting claims to political-legal legitimacy based on such reasoning. If to this we add suspicions about the general instability and malleability of interpretation based on moral reasoning; place this issue in the context of the complex, discretion-based administrative state, and suggest that this latter organisational form opportunistically seizes on the 'deformalising' tendencies of 'idealist' or natural law thinking in opposition to the generality and predictability of a formalist or proceduralist conception of the Rule of Law, we then have the basic ingredients for a powerful rejection of the aspiration to construct and defend a moral conception of the idea of legal validity.

The second feature is a belief in democracy as an inherently liberating process which should guide our quest for the good society and, hence, the basis of a critique of the existing state of affairs. In this idea of democratic government, central to the critical account is the establishment of a strong link between, on the one hand, 'the will of the people', and, on the other, law and government policy. Combining these two sets of assumptions, it appears that any weakening of the democratic process by a legal theory which envisages the incorporation of a moral-critical function into the legal system itself is unacceptable. Rather, the intrusion of moral reasoning will be seen as producing a 'democratic deficit', in that the moral ideology of a bureaucratic or judicial elite will inhibit or frustrate the will of the people.

grassroots of society and the state apparatus, between the "people" and the political functionaries, and between legislation and law enforcement.

At p. 871–2 she elaborates on this when she says that Habermas, Jurgen *Faktizitat und Geltung*, (Frankfurt am Main, Suhrkamp, 1992):

'leaves the assymetries of the radical conception of popular sovereignty behind it. Since according to that radical conception all controls can only be exercised 'from below', unjust decisions by a parliament should only be corrected by a critical public, and indeed, not "from above" by a constitutional court.'

This is a plausible and not inaccurate picture of the tendencies and inadequacies of the ideological function of the Rule of Law in the modern state; a picture which over several decades has been sketched out in increasingly illuminating detail by social and political theorists as well as the more imaginative public lawyers.[4] In Maus's critique, the account comprises three central components. The first is the analysis and critique of the Rule of Law subsequent to the emergence of the modern administrative state. This argument arises directly from her acknowledgement of the value of Carl Schmitt's now topical[5] and partially rehabilitated critique of the constitutional degeneration of liberal democracy into the 'pluralism' of the Weimar situation. The second is the defence of a concept of strong or direct democracy as the legitimating ground of the legislative power of the modern state (arising from her understandable disagreement with Schmitt's theoretical defence of plebiscitary dictatorship as the optimum 'solution' to the Weimar problem). Finally, there is the attempt to characterise legal form and procedure as the fundamental safeguard of liberty as opposed to 'morality', which is presented as necessarily antithetical to democracy and, consequently, antithetical to legal validity. This is an argument which Maus relates to Kant's distinction between law and morals, and attempts to show that Kant's own conception of an individualised (or monological) moral reason based on the intuitions of autonomy and equality, when taken as a ground for *legal* validity, militates against the necessarily *dialogical* or communicative, participatory, consensus-building processes required by the attempt to fashion a legitimate and *pluralist* society.

---

[4] See e.g. Tony Prosser's important piece from 1982 which attempts to reconceptualise traditional approaches: 'Towards a Critical Public Law' (1982) 9 *Journal of Law and Society*; also the convenient layout of comparative responses to regulatory and distributive issues in Craig, Paul P., *Administrative Law* (3rd edn., Sweet and Maxwell, London, 1994); and the essays of Lewis, N.D. *et al.* in Jowell, J., and Oliver, D., *The Changing Constitution* (2nd edn., Clarendon Press, Oxford, 1989).

[5] See, e.g., the *CJLJ* (n. 1 *supra*) devoted to Schmitt.

This latter is the hub of a debate which starts, perhaps, with Kant, but moves towards a more recent position which seems to create more problems than it solves. That is, much modern liberal thought wishes to reject Kant's insistence on the basis of the moral law as being founded on the individual's insight into the objective freedom (autonomy) and equality of the rational will, and replace this crucial thesis in Kant with one or another version of ethical indeterminacy or moral pluralism. However, there appears in much contemporary political philosophy a widespread desire to retain, simultaneously, the foundational Kantian values of individual freedom and equality, whilst celebrating both cultural diversity and a reverence for the imaginative construction of individual identities. This sounds like a fairly straightforward 'liberal' approach to political philosophy; but the attempt to overcome the theoretical and actual tensions of these three axioms of modern political understanding is perhaps the central preoccupation of modern and post-modern political discourse. We think that the project of articulating a non-moral conception of democracy to overcome the spectre of Kantian individualist or 'monological' morality must circumscribe its own 'dialogical' prescriptions in rather monological ways. Maus, therefore, presents us with an opportunity to discuss an important and potentially wide-ranging problem which ultimately resolves into the question of how democracy—or some form of social consensus—both creates and yet might be restrained or resisted by a morally rational conception of law. We will attempt to address it in the order presented above, concentrating first on the influence of Schmitt's critique of pluralism.

Weber, Schmitt and 'Disenchantment'

We might begin with the Weberian model of modern society which served as a background to Schmitt's analysis of pluralist democracy in Weimar. Weber, like other late nineteenth-century neo-Kantian jurists and social theorists, accepted that the 'moral unity' of pre-modern or traditional society, and with it the charismatics of leadership, had necessarily given way to a new form of rational-technical social organisation. There was substantial disagreement, however, about whether this unity was either recoverable or self-evidently desirable. Weber's posture of value-neutrality and political detachment creates ambiguity about his views in this regard, although methodologically, as we noted in Chapter 3, he was highly critical of the historical-nationalistic ontology propounded by the Heidelberg scholars of the generation before him.[6] Rather, he saw societal development and forms of political association now accommodating, and striving to remain consonant with, the spread and cultivation of an emergent individualism and interest pluralism which he saw as the result of the natural evolution and fragmentation of the division of labour arising from industrialism, technological advance and the growth of markets.

In Weber's theory, famously and ideal-typically, the unity of traditional values is replaced by a 'disenchanted' scientific-technical ethos. The strengthening of the idea of representative democracy, individualism and value and interest pluralism appeared to imply opposition to, and the eradication of, institutions raised as monuments to rigidified tradition. It appears, therefore, as perfectly understandable that we find in Weber, Kelsen and Radbruch, and later in Hart, opposition to the idea that an anachronistic or metaphysical conception of 'the good' might inform legislative and judical processes contrary to the formal-rational and technical-administrative strivings of modern society. Thus by moving our focus from the co-ordinatory logic of the Autonomy Thesis (see Chapter 2 *supra*) to the need for a political dynamic, we can understand the fairly straightforward promulgation of the correspondingly formal-rational thesis of Legal Positivism (in Weber's theory, a Legal Formalism[7]) as a progressive response to the legacy of moral tradition.

---

[6] See Weber, Max, *Roscher and Knies: The Logical Problem of Historical Economics* (Free Press, New York, 1975).

[7] See Weber, Max, *The Theory of Social and Economic Organisation* (Oxford University Press, New York, 1947), 154–6; and also his *Staatssoziologie* (Duncker Humboldt, Berlin, 1956), 99.

Sharing broadly these Weberian premises concerning the analysis of pluralist development and the modern bureaucratic, technical-administrative state, the work of Carl Schmitt takes a curious turn in respect of the prognosis for democracy. Where the Weberian thesis almost defines the possibility of democracy as the existence of interest and value-complexity in a 'neutral' (formal-rational) legal order overriding the homogeneity of moral tradition, Schmitt attacks as *un*democratic the very existence of interest pluralism allied to what he saw as the serious incongruity of the once *legitimate*, but now *legitimating*, ideology of the state: the Rule of Law. By 'Rule of Law', and according to Schmitt, we are to understand the ideal of the state dominated by a legislature democratically committed to the idea of calculability, predictability and generality of laws pursuant to rational parliamentary debate; an ideal which derives its legitimacy from its optimal congruity with the well-being of a society alleged to be more or less culturally homogeneous.[8]

Briefly, Schmitt saw the growth and fragmentation of sectional interests and the rise of the administrative state as the decline of the *nation* state and the severing of the link between the people (*Volk*) and the government. Particularly, in the context of Weimar, he saw disparate interest blocs manœuvring in the world of parliamentary politics, forming larger, pragmatic party alliances and abusing the machinery of political representation to secure power. Once established, executive elites, legitimated by the ideology of the Rule of Law, and most importantly on the basis of a legitimating welfarist ethic based on an indeterminate conception of some future 'public good', use the financial resources of the unaccountable and bureaucratically inscrutable

[8] These ideas are presented in Schmitt's various works, but see particularly, Schmitt, Carl, *The Concept of the Political* (Schwab G. (ed.), Lomax, H. (trans.), University of Chicago Press, Chicago, Ill., 1996); also *Der Hüter der Verfassung* (Berlin, Duncker Humboldt, 1931); and 'Legalität und Legitimität' (München 1932). For important references and analysis see *CJLJ* (n. 1 *supra*), particularly Mehring, Richard, at 105–7; Leydet, Dominique, at 49–52; and Howse, Robert, 'From Legitmacy to Dictatorship—and Back again: Leo Strauss's Critique of the Anti-Liberalism of Carl Schmitt', 77–103, especially footnotes and wider references.

administration as a repository of largesse to secure political support from targeted sections of the electorate and other organised interest groups. According to Schmitt, the allegedly shared understandings and basic homogeneity of the nineteenth-century (particularly British) model of elected representatives in government and opposition, amenable to rational persuasion and forming a sovereign legislature issuing general laws, no longer obtained.[9] This, we must note, was not then, and is not now, an uncommon or particularly original view of the shortcomings of the democratic ideal in the context of the complex administrative state. However, Schmitt's understanding of the ideal is of exceptional interest and differs from most modern liberal responses to the generally accepted problem of pluralist complexity. Let us pursue it in more detail.

First, let us note with Dominique Leydet that Schmitt, from the outset, defines pluralism as 'a situation in which the state has become dependent upon, or subordinate to, the various social and economic associations that make up contemporary industrial societies'.[10] This situation is not self-evidently undesirable. However, in the context of Schmitt's analysis of state and society it is to be understood as the pathological expression of the failure of a complex structure of social and economic institutions. This is important in that Schmitt's analysis of the nature of 'pluralist' society is pivotal to his critique of democracy and legitimacy, for the term as he employs it has a certain ambiguity which requires careful articulation.

Schmitt saw pluralism not as the mere existence of disparate and fragmented interests in society (a sociological conception which is merely a corollary of the very idea of a complex division of labour) but loads it heavily and perjoratively with a 'welfarist' ideology arising from his conception, to which we will presently turn, of the 'anti-political' 'metaphysics of liberalism' and the very specific features of what contemporary public lawyers would recognise as a model of modern and virulent 'cor-

[9] See Leydet (n. 1 *supra*), 53.

[10] *Ibid.*, 49: here Leydet translates and quotes from Schmitt's 'Staatsethik und pluralistischer Staat' (1930) XXXV *Kant-Studien* 28 at 31.

poratist' government. For Schmitt, interest-differentiation *per se* is seen as a developmental and structural instability. Its political expression, pluralism, must, it seems, necessarily descend into a 'welfarist' pathology which precipitates a constitutional degeneration into what he refers to famously as the ethic of *pacta sunt servanda*. This is the situation in which parliamentary groupings effectively hijack the state and use its authority and largesse in pursuit of short-term sectional interest. Constitutional 'guarantees' under this arrangement become identical with whatever pragmatic alliances and rules of the political game happen to be agreed between the incumbent interest blocs. This, not surprisingly, he regarded as destructive of the unity and integrity of the V*olk*.

We come then to the crux of the matter in respect of Schmitt's conception of democracy. Schmitt's response to this process of disintegration involved two things. First, in his role as a principled Conservative Nationalist, Schmitt interpreted his duty as safeguarding the constitution from the unruly invasion and usurpation of parliament by anti-democratic forces. In the recurrent parliamentary crises of the Weimar Republic, this meant providing a jurisprudential justification for the interpretation of the crucial Article 48 of the Weimar Constitution as offering an absolutist prerogative to the incumbent chancellor in times of national emergency. This view is neither uncommon nor illiberal: it operates on the premise that democracy and democratic representation logically cannot extend its freedoms and protections to forces which seek to exploit these privileges to destroy democracy itself. Bendersky's immensely readable biography presents Schmitt as a resourceful and tireless defender of the constitution in this regard.[11]

After 1933, however, with the advent of Hitler as Chancellor, Schmitt rounds viciously on the very basis of the ideas of constitutional liberalism. By 1934 we see him propagating the idea that the legitimacy of the the Third Reich is embodied in the will of the Führer; a Führer defined as the personification of the

[11] Bendersky, Joseph W., *Carl Schmitt: Theorist for the Reich* (Princeton University Press, Princeton, NJ, 1983).

constitutionally unquestionable, infallible and irresistible Will of the sovereign *Volk*. In a situation in which the integral identity of the *Volk* is endangered—what Schmitt called 'the state of exception'—the validity of a decision arises solely from the moral courage of a spiritually gifted leader of the *Volk* to affirm its Will to Power. Such pronouncements are *ipso facto*, for Schmitt, an expression of the democratic will of the people.[12]

This inverted view of democratic representation was hardly original, stemming as it did from the ideas of French revolutionary writers, and their analysis of the sovereignty of the people as the genuine *pouvoir constituant* unbounded by constitutional principle in their right to assert and defend their identity. The logic of this lies in the idea, contrary to modern critical approaches in constitutional and administrative law, that it is not so much the need to monitor and control the *outputs* of government (that is, laws, policy, delegated authority and, hence, bureaucratic discretionary power) but, rather, to 'democratise' the range of *inputs* by homogenising and unifying the 'interests of the people' by rescuing them from their ideologically fragmented condition. If the 'interests of the people' can simultaneously be gleaned, expressed and automatically translated into law by and through the spon-

---

[12] Schmitt develops these views in *The Concept of the Political* and in *Political Theology: Four Chapters on the Concept of Sovereignty* (Schwab G. (trans.), MIT Press, Cambridge, Mass., 1985). See invaluable discussions, however, in Howse (n. 8 *supra*) and in Holmes, S., *The Anatomy of Anti-Liberalism* (University of Chicago Press, Chicago, Ill., 1993). The idea of 'decisionism', and Hobbesian support for it, he develops in *Die Diktatur* (Duncker and Humboldt, Munich, 1928) esp. 21–4, and see on this matter, importantly, Christi, Renato, *CJLJ* (n. 1 *supra*), 189ff. Of this view, Howse says:

'Schmitt deviates from Machiavelli in a crucial respect—he admires the resolve and honesty of a self confident dictatorship, not domination as such. He seeks therefore, not a combination of the lion and the fox, but rather a Cesare with the soul of Luther. Thus when in *Political Theology*, Schmitt refers to the "exacting moral decision" as the "core of the political idea", this does not refer to the aspiration to ground decisionism in a higher morality—what is morally exacting is the requirement to decide "out of nothingess". Moral exactness means nothing more or less that the courage and honesty to affirm one's own will to power as the only ground of the decision'—Howse, R., 'From Legitimacy to Dictatorship and Back Again' (n. 1. *supra*), 80.

taneous will of one person, this is indeed the swiftest and surest form of 'democracy'. But this historically catastrophic 'solution' to the problem of pluralist democracy is, of course, the aspect of Schmitt's analysis from which his recent expositors are anxious to distance themselves.[13] If, however, Schmitt is thought to be somewhere on the right track with his critique of pluralist elites abusing the principle of the Rule of Law in the 'social' state, what alternative is there to his gruesome solution in the shape of his conception of 'direct' democracy, or more accurately, a plebiscitary dictatorship? Does the problem lie with pluralism and complexity, or the moralisation or 'deformalisation' of the law which appears to arise from pluralism?

Pluralism, for Schmitt, in any form, and for the reasons we will explain below, is inherently unstable. This is important, because any attempt to glean from Schmitt a sensible understanding of the problems of the modern pluralist state, and especially an insight into how one might improve the quality of democracy in it, requires, in our view, a complete rejection of his basic sociological and political concepts. Schmitt's antipathy to pluralism is better understood as the obverse of his attachment, common in much nineteenth-century German sociological and historical thought, to the idea of the existence of historical bonds of homogeneous interests alleged to be manifest in the rise and flourishing of nations. Nations, for Schmitt, are necessarily and essentially friend/foe groupings. These divisions arise naturally and automatically from our essential nature and are beyond rational grasp. Once constituted, the group becomes a political entity in what, for Schmitt, is the very essence of the word 'political'—i.e. they are entities prepared to fight for their sovereign integrity and identity. The wishes and fears of a nation as constituted by the *Volk* or 'the People' are infallible and beyond any *artificial* (i.e. constitutional) restraint. *Genuine* political struggle and decision-making arise from, and consist in, this dangerous and serious enterprise of the preservation of the pure

[13] See e.g. Mouffe, Chantal, 'Carl Schmitt and the Paradox of Liberal Democracy' *CJLJ* (n. 1 *supra*), 5–21; also Maus, Ingeborg, 'The 1933 Break in Carl Schmitt's Theory' (*ibid.*), 125–41.

and homogeneous identity of the community or *Volk*. The interests of the *Volk* are not so much identified by deliberative reflection on the part of individuals; rather, they are articulated by
great leaders possessed of an immense insight into the *Volksgeist*
or authentic spirit of the people.[14]

Liberalism, by contrast, and according to Schmitt, is the
degenerate enterprise of disguising and obscuring this reality, i.e.
the 'seriousness of life', by attempting to portray humanity as an
undifferentiated entity capable of unity and harmony in a discourse which admits and respects the essentially relativistic, and
thus essentially equal, validity of all values. Not unlike Marx,
Schmitt also emphasises the reduction of life to economics and
'entertainment'. *Pluralism* is the triumph of this 'anti-human'
ideology in realising the political, economic and cultural condition whereby the soul of the *Volk* is fragmented, and thus the
will of the *Volk* or 'the People' is repressed. A pluralist carve-up
of resources and political privilege masquerading as a liberal
constitution is, then, an affront to democracy; its violent
destruction by the resurrection and reassertion of the Spirit of
the People or *Volksgeist* can be seen as undemocratic only from
the perverse perspective of the liberal ethic of 'relative rationalism'—a pluralistic talking shop manipulated by elites.

This ideal conception of a *direct* link between the will of the
people and the law was not novel in Schmitt's time. Rather it had
been propounded by one of the most celebrated German jurists
of the nineteenth century, Ferdinand von Savigny.[15] Savigny,
drew up a legal theory based on the idea that the very existence,
origin and concept of law is derived from the will of the people—
the common will. The common will was identified via the
cultural institutions of society which, in turn, were seen as expressions of the historical development of the people's identity.

[14] This is the general thesis of Schmitt's *The Concept of the Political*—see n. 8
supra.

[15] An accessible discussion of Savigny is to be found in Freeman, M.A. (ed.),
Lloyd's Introduction to Jurisprudence (6th edn., Sweet and Maxwell, London,
1994), 799–804.

The law is one such cultural institution and the positive demands that flow from it must be interpreted as expressions of the *Volksgeist*. Likewise, the state represents the abstract materialisation of the will of the people. This theory of law, later to be amended by German jurists such as Ihering and Puchta, seems to have led Carl Schmitt to his particular theory of the interpretation and application of posited law.

Schmitt, again after 1933, propounded the value of a 'situationist' and 'decisionist' theory of law which has much in common with post-modern views on the matter. The idea, integral to Schmitt's metaphysics of the sovereign *Volk*, is that a posited norm admits of a range of possible applications, but arguing about *constitutional* limits to the interpretation of laws is, says Schmitt, obfuscation inherent in the ideology of liberal jurisprudence. In the spirit of Savigny, Schmitt asserts that interpretations of legal norms must draw on the normative potential of the *Volksgeist* particularly in the acute 'state of exception' or crisis, where the *Volk* (as manifested in the will of the Führer) seeks to assert or defend its identity. It is in this crisis phase that the *Volk* must assert the friend/foe relationship and decide who or what are to be included or excluded as members of the social entity. The crisis precipitates the decision, and the decision cannot recognise any prior juridical limits. The identification and *a fortiori*, the *legitimation* of a norm cannot, therefore, exist prior to its concrete application in specific and unique circumstances. This is the Schmittian origin of the idea of 'dynamic' or 'deformalised' law. Thus, ingeniously, we see in Schmitt the apparently consistent presentation of the concept of democracy in the form of the very antithesis of its modern, pluralistic expression. Ostensibly, then, the Schmittian critique of pluralism is about a defecit in democracy.

Constitutionalism in Pluralist Society

But just how far can the conceptual articulation of any plausible contemporary critique of government and administration remain coterminous with Schmitt's conceptual apparatus? The metaphysics of the philosophy of history, which, as Weber usefully observed, might be subsumed generically under the label of 'emanatism'[16] are fascinating, if rationally unfathomable, but subscribing to it in any form strongly presupposes a pessimism about the development of economic, cultural and religious diversity. They are thus perfectly apposite to the increasing extremes of Schmitt's conservative nationalism. The bottom line is that sovereignty lies with the people and the law is the expression of its will. There is no *legal* power to limit the expression of that will. It is important therefore, that we examine just how far Ingeborg Maus' critique of a moralised concept of law is rooted in Savigny's and Schmitt's rejection of the attempt to impose constitutional—or moral-legal-limits on the will of 'the people' or its 'infallible' representatives. Clearly, she sees a general and continuing validity in Schmitt's analysis. She says[17]:

> Schmitt found the cause of the functional problems of modern parliaments in the necessary adaptation of state activity and the legal structure to the changed economic conditions of the twentieth century. The state's engagement in permanent economic crisis management requires possibilities for intervention which are situation-bound and oriented to single cases. And that brings the state into conflict with its bond to 'standing' and general laws—that is, the outputs of parliament.

She goes on to say:

> This idea of a dynamic and deformalized law for which Schmitt gave a theoretical foundation is today what we have in practice in all spheres of the law. At present, constitutional courts, especially that of the Federal Republic, use methods of interpretation in all spheres which permit them to determine the content of the constitution in accordance with the pending individual case . . . The constitution is no longer the normative standard by which citizens can measure the conformity of state conduct to the constitution. On the contrary, it serves to empower and legitimate the state apparatus in programming itself.

[16] See n. 6 *supra*.
[17] Maus (n. 13 *supra*), 126.

We see expressed, as in Schmitt, an apparent faith in the idea of a Golden Age of the Rule of Law where democratically elected representatives are faithful to the wishes of the people and all are secure in the bounded calculability and predictability of the law. Things go wrong, however, when, with the coming of the modern social state, 'the positive criteria' for judical decisions are set aside, or 'single case', situation-specific crisis measures are taken, or when the legislature empowers its administrators to 'negotiate' the law with industrialists. Maus is right to point out the problematic nature of these developments *vis-à-vis* democratic accountability, but we think at this point that we should query the apparent convergence of Schmitt's anxieties with the concerns of contemporary constitutional scholarship. In the following passage, when Maus speaks of moral concepts, is she talking about the welfare state's disingenuous ethic of 'relative rationalism' to which Schmitt counterposed his philosophy of history and the myth of the *Volk*? Is she endorsing Schmitt's analysis of the strategy of liberal jurisprudence to disguise the foundationless, reasonless, infinitely indeterminate nature of all rule or, rather, is she speaking of the inevitability of the mundane, but nevertheless sensible, presumption that as contextualisation and complexity breed discretion, discretion must obviously be exercised with integrity and for the common good—and that the conception of the common good is a contentious *moral* notion giving rise to problems of interpretation? Let us remind ourselves of the point. Maus says:[18]

it is precisely the direct integration of *moral principle* into the concept of law which breaks down the limits of law and thus removes the limits to state regulation.

The problem she associates here with 'moralisation' is that under this arrangement, by asking judges and officials to interpret acts of the legislature according to a criterion of moral legitimacy as a precondition of legal validity, we introduce an unstable and potentially uncontrollable dimension to the legitimation or rejection of legislation which goes beyond the

[18] Maus, 1988 (n. 2 *supra*), 141–2, our emphasis.

classically conceived democratic intentions of constitutional legitimation.[19]

Morality, then, allows officials in the legal system either to uphold or set aside prior political (i.e. popular mandate) decisions as they please. Since there is no criterion determining the choice between moral and democratic legitimation, there can be no extra-legal control of the legitimacy of legal decisions. The decision-making bodies may choose whatever ground is convenient for the furthering of their own interests in the overall struggle for power within the state apparatus. This is the Schmittian situation *par excellence*, and as described would, of course, be irrational and intolerable.

Constitutionalism and Democracy

What we can infer from this is that the fear of the 'democratic defecit' must be based on aspects of the general idea that constitutional provisions cannot, in principle, restrain the diversity and ingenuity of interpretative strategies based on moral rationality. We have noted three central objections: (a) the concern about the general instability of interpretation based on moral reasoning; (b) the effective delimitation of the boundaries of law and constitution stemming from the malleability of moral reasoning; and (c) the emasculation of an extra-systemic source of moral restraint on popular democracy by the incorporation of the moral-critical function into the legal system itself. But it might be wise at this point to step back from, or perhaps even jettison, Schmitt's dazzling analysis of pluralist pathology, his concept of the radical indeterminacy of legal systems and the related thesis of the 'decision out of nothingness'. For although there is most certainly a need to attend to the structural inadequacies of the modern pluralist state, we are in danger of missing a more obvious source of the problem. Let us consider two options.

[19] See a defence of Maus's views in Ericsson, Lars 'Rätten och Moralen" (1990) 48, *Retfærd* 10.

First, if we interpret Maus as suggesting that Schmitt's oppor-
tunist critique of Weimar pluralism is relevant to our task as
public lawyers today, then we must also retrace and incorporate
his metaphysical opposition to the very core of the notion of
liberalism. This, as we have clearly—if very briefly—outlined
above, states that liberalism, in the form of the classical conception of the Rule of Law, is fundamentally incompatible with
democracy because of an ideology of formal equality—i.e. the
metaphysics of 'relative rationalism'—which seeks to destroy
'the political' and replace it with 'the economic' and so forth.
The *moralisation* of law, for Schmitt, means the *obfuscation* of
law in the pursuit of a *Weltanschauung* of liberal metaphysics—
not merely the unexceptionable yet admirable commonplace
that judges and administrators should act at least in accordance
with 'the public good' or in 'good faith'. Schmitt is right, of
course, as his incisive opponent Leo Strauss noted, in castigat-
ing the ethical relativism of liberals: that ideas about acting in
good faith presuppose faith to some foundational principle of
common good.[20] But this is merely hot air in Schmitt, for his
characterisation of the *demos* as a *Volk*, and consequently his
ideas of plebiscitary democracy, do not even engage with the
problem of stable interpretation: all interpretation and application for Schmitt is—*a priori*—decisionistic and ideological. Thus
whatever occurred in Weimar constitutionally, legislatively or
administratively, or indeed in any pluralist administration,
would, for him, have been an 'undemocratic' carve-up between
the degenerate, incumbent elites.

Secondly, if we are concerned, as Maus is, to present a plea
for increased democracy, then rejecting the superstitious and
contradictory excesses of Schmitt in the shape of the *Führer*
principle, we must now say what is envisaged by a workable
form of pluralist democratic input into the legislative and administrative process. From here, retaining our reservations about the
indeterminacy and malleability of moral reason, we might then
deal with Maus's misgivings in this regard as perhaps a

[20] See this important piece, 'Notes on Carl Schmitt', in the appendix to
Schmitt's *Concept of the Political* (n. 8 *supra*).

Radbruchian or Hartian claim for the optimisation of determinacy and the structuring of 'strong' discretion in judicial and administrative interpretation. In this way, the problem of interpretation becomes at least clear.

But we must say at this point that we suspect that the problem of interpretation in relation to any conception of social purpose will prove to be beyond the scope of direct (popular) democracy, irrationalism, relativism or positivism of any hue. For the fact of the matter is that the problem of interpretation, that is, the problem of a greater or lesser degree of indeterminacy of scope of a posited norm, stays with us in its complexity even if we are able to avail ourselves of objective moral principles *and* an essentially coherent concept of liberal *pluralist* democracy. The desire for calculability and restraint, concern for subjective right and so on is a constitutional question of the moral boundaries of legal interpretation and, as we suggested in our introduction and throughout our previous discussions, this boils down to the issue of whether or not we can avail ourselves of a stable account of the indirect application of legitimate foundational principles in complex circumstances. We might refer to these *equally and interchangeably* as either 'moral' or 'democratic' principles. Hence, our efforts should be directed to the logic of this definitive stage of the judicial process, that is, the relationship between sovereignty, legislative power and legitimate (i.e. in Maus's terms, democratic) application of the law. The difficulties of stable interpretation of principled norms in complex democratic or 'open' societies is a basic jurisprudential issue; it is, perhaps, definitive of the discipline. It is important, therefore, that Schmitt's formulation of the problem is not assimilated to, and presented as, a progressive form of Legal Positivism which we find, for example, in Radbruch or Hart.

Discretion, Democracy and the Rule of Law

In Chapters 2 and 3 we considered the basic problem of social organisation: the problem of cohesion, decision making, dispute resolution and the allocation of an authoritative 'say'. Sociologically, we can agree that all these tasks must be performed as preconditions of the continuing existence of a group—however large or small—that is, they must be performed *somehow*. The question, as we pointed out in detail in Chapter 3, is precisely *how*, and *to what ends*. This at once poses the problems of procedural and substantive legitimacy and points to the issue of the function and extent of general participation by those subject to normative constraints—legal, moral or otherwise—in rule and policy-making. This much is true of any socio-economic formation.

The idea that an authoritative sovereign subject to the Rule of Law is the precondition of our advance from a 'state of nature' is perhaps a contentious and extravagant, if useful, figure; but the emergence of regulatory forms of the *public* and the *positive*[21] as a feature of the move from simple to complex forms of the division of labour is not. The Rule of Law is a broad expression of the change from habitual and customary interaction to codified and positively promulgated regulation. Concomitant to the idea of authoritative and integrative decision-making is the problem of the universality (at least within any particular society) of obligation. The diversity of interests and thus the complexity of the ends of law, and the increasing notion of the technical and pragmatic desirability of representation and participation present us with the challenge of the notion of integrative democracy. Let us try to clarify not so much the richness and complexity of these ideas as the bare minimum for our purposes here, which, we must remember, concern the nature, scope and desirability or otherwise of the intrusion of moral reasoning into processes of legal reasoning. Let us also remember that the basic premises of Schmitt and Maus's critique of the role of moral reasoning in law are, simultaneously, implicit endorsements of the value and legitimacy of the idea of the Rule of Law, and the values of constitutional democracy. But are these institutions mutually and *self-evidently* supportive?

---

[21] See Unger, Roberto M., *Law in Modern Society* (The Free Press, New York, 1976), Chap. 2.

We are happy to concur with E.P. Thompson's point, heretical in orthodox Marxism, that the idea or the ideal of the Rule of Law is 'an unqualified human good'.[22] But, historically, the usage and application of the term has often been ambiguous and occasionally banal. At best we must realise that the idea of the Rule of Law is a noble aspiration and not a set of instructions on how to achieve those aspirations. Let us be clear about the rich intent, yet the meagre substance, of the concept of the Rule of Law. K.C. Davies' observations are refreshingly phlegmatic in this matter. Jurisprudence, he says, reacts to the problem of discretionary power (e.g. interpretation of statutes, adjudication of lawful administration, decisions to refrain from prosecution, and so on) through a 'vague idea known as the Rule of Law or the supremacy of law'. He says[23]:

> The concept has many meanings, and in some of its meanings it is highly beneficial and widely accepted. For instance, in international relations the idea or the ideal of the Rule of Law means that law should in great measure replace use of force; . . . Similarly, in domestic affairs, one version of the Rule of Law is that a system of rule by law is to be preferred to a system of private use of force. Almost everyone agrees with Aristotle's statement that 'The Rule of Law is preferable to that of any individual.' . . .
>
> The historical subordination of the king to law—to what a parliament enacts or to the law declared by judges—can be regarded as a victory for the Rule of Law. This sense of the Rule of Law is about the same as the concept of government under law, or what Aristotle and others and finally the Massachusetts constitution called a 'government of laws and not of men'. The idea shades into such concepts as due process, natural law, higher law, democracy and fairness, absence of arbitrariness. Hardly anyone can oppose such vagueness in the abstract, opposition develops only when concrete meaning is put into such concepts.

It would be wise to maintain this cautious tone throughout the remainder of our discussion. For 'the Rule of Law' is a slogan

[22] Thompson, E.P., *Whigs and Hunters* (Harmondsworth, Penguin Books, Random House, 1975), 259–69.

[23] Davies, Kenneth Culp, *Discretionary Justice* (University of Illinois Press, Urbana, Ill., 1979), 28.

which can metamorphose from Aristotelian visions of the *telos* of rational humanity to the bureaucratic emptiness of calls for procedure for the sake of procedure, to pleas for restraint in political protest or industrial action, through to appeals for obedience to the most grotesque forms of injustice. If the idea is about *equality* before the law and about the *generality* and *consistency* of application, then this is about the idea of reason and universality in law, and again we welcome the idea. But if the defence of the Rule of Law is taken to be a substantial element of the aspirations of democracy, then we must say a lot more about the rationality which is alleged to inhere in both of these potentially complex ideas.

The classical response of political philosophy to the problem of order in, for example, Hobbes and Locke, is to institute a sovereign power for the promotion of peace and individual security based upon a social contract. The limits to the sovereign's power, and thus the extent of our duty to obey, are the main bone of contention between Hobbes and Locke, and so too in Rousseau, who ironically and curiously has at once the most *participatory* democratic conception—one which is easily assimilable to the ideas of Habermas—and yet one that is not implausibly interpreted as a defence of the philosopher king and law-giver and, perhaps, to the theory of V*olksgeist*.[24] Complex as these arguments are in Rousseau, we can say that once the

[24] We refer, of course, to the idea of the General Will. For the General Will is not merely the majority vote—the General Will might be in opposition to the majority vote—it might even be, as Rousseau himself suggested, the will of *one person* seen as a conduit for the will of all. In Rousseau, too, 'the people' (not the disparate multitude) are sovereign and 'the people' alone give law. However, 'the people' is not identical with 'the legislator', nor are parliaments regarded as legislatively competent; they are merely executors of the will of 'the people'. But in Rousseau 'the people' can issue law only in accordance with the General Will. Thus, the attempt to assimilate Rousseau to the cause of 'popular' democracy gives rise to the problem that democracy might not be particularly 'democratic'. See Rousseau, J.J., *The Social Contract and Discourses* (G.D.H. Cole (ed.), London, Dent, Everyman, 1983), particularly Book 2, *III*, on 'Whether the General Will is Fallible', *VII*, 'The Legislator' and *VIII*, 'The People'. See also our discussion in 'Idealism for Pragmatists', in *Archiv für Recht und Sozialphilosophie* 4/99.

notion of 'popular' democracy is divorced from the seductive but, in this context, unhelpful ideas of majoritarianism or unqualified consensus, articulating the legitimating properties of this particular form of political and legislative will-formation becomes extremely demanding.

Let us consider a few options. Democracy can be taken as (i) the majority vote-giving, power-investing function of the people—without redress—to a sovereign legislature, or (ii) the majority vote plus the opportunity for ongoing participation and scrutiny of the legislature, or (iii), all that, plus a constitutional set of parameters concerning the 'public good' or the 'rights of man'; further, it could be (iv), the morally and rationally attenuated will of the people as expressed in the immanent values of its historical institutions (i.e. a version of Savigny, or, plausibly, a condensed but not unreasonable rendition of Dworkin) or (v), as is clearly Carl Schmitt's view, guaranteeing that the general interests of the sovereign nation are infalllibly served by ensuring that someone is empowered to witness, articulate and implement law in accordance with the spiritual destiny of the *Volk*. Whichever model is chosen—and there are obviously many more versions available than these noted—the idea cannot be posited unproblematically as the self-evident, legitimating ground of all interpretation of laws; for the scope and limits of legitimate decision are immanent in the *concept* of democracy, and democracy in practice is quite capable of embroiling itself in all sorts of reflexive contradictions. One such is the hypothetically perennial (and historically commonplace) example of the election of candidates and whole parties fundamentally opposed to the process of universal suffrage and equality of participation rights in political debate. Further, a legislative body might well be properly constituted by some form of elective procedure plausibly termed 'democratic', and we might further assume that the electors had some knowledge of their own 'real' and stated interests, and even that the legislature might legislate in accordance with those interests. However, legislation is issued in one context of interests and circumstances and might well be interpreted and applied in another; one would then have to interpret the validity of law relative to judgements about the validity of historical, economic and political context. In addition, if we take into account the kind of pluralist complexity which features as the basis of Schmitt's or Maus's critique, a powerful executive constituting in effect the majority of the legislature might empower all manner of agencies to administer certain policies at their discretion. This, of course is increasingly a feature of the modern situation. But if this is seen as unacceptable, or an attack on the Rule of Law, it is not because of the lack of propriety of the make-up of the legislature, or of the executive; nor the unavoidable requirement to delegate power and discretion to administrators; it is because, according to Schmitt and Maus, the interpretation and application of the laws and of administrative decision-making are seen to be beyond 'democratic' constraint. This can only mean, however, that interpretation and application involve *value-judgements* which are not referred back in every case to what must be seen as a representative parliament or, perhaps, the electorate itself.[25]

Thus two questions now arise following the perception that the Rule of Law ideal has been undermined by arbitrary or 'illegal' or 'unconstitutional' interpretation. First, what would we advise the judge to do in response to the complaint that, say, an administrative body had acted unfairly; that is, had acted on its powers of discretion but employed values which were considered to be unacceptable (undemocratic)? The closest we come to an answer in Maus's writings is her expressed agreement with Weimar constitutional theorists Gerhard Anschütz and Richard Thoma whom, according to Maus, claimed that[26]:

> all interventions in the rights of citizens were subject to statute law and therefore 'null and void' without the consent of the people's

[25] This to-and-fro process is actually characteristic of post-revolutionary French practice where the judiciary were instructed to submit their interpretations back to parliament to be vetted. See Alec Stone's important anlysis in *The Birth of Judicial Politics in France* (Oxford University Press, Oxford, 1992), 23–30.

[26] Maus, 1988 (n. 2 *supra*), 160–1.

representatives; laws were, by definition, 'all, but also only' those laws passed with the consent of the people's representatives.

But this does not seem to be helpful when the problem we face is an interpretive one. What we need is a response alert to the genuine proportions of the issue in hand. But let us give this broadly positivistic view the full advantage of the assumption of a Hartian positive order. Let us assume that we have a separation of powers in respect of legislature, executive and judiciary. Let us assume that we are of the opinion that mixing up morality with legality is a mistake. Herbert Hart—certainly no advocate of the moralisation of law—gives this perfectly clear response. He says[27]:

> Judicial decision, especially on matters of high constitutional import, often involves a choice between moral values, and not merely the application of some single outstanding moral principle; for it is folly to believe that where the meaning of the law is in doubt, morality always has a clear answer to offer. At this point judges may again make a choice which is neither arbitrary nor mechanical; and here often display characteristic judicial virtues, the special appropriateness of which to legal decision explains why some feel reluctant to call such judicial activity 'legislative'. These virtues are: impartiality and neutrality in surveying the alternatives; consideration for the interests of all who will be affected; and a concern to deploy some acceptable general principle as a reasoned basis for decision. No doubt because a plurality of such principles is always possible it cannot be *demonstrated* that a decision is uniquely correct: but it may be made acceptable as the reasoned product of informed impartial choice. In all this we have the 'weighing' and 'balancing' characteristic of the effort to do justice between competing interests.

We can certainly agree with this sober suggestion. Our second question, then, is: *what are the interests which should be balanced, and upon what criteria are they to be weighed?*

If it is really the case that these questions can be answered by a determinate, bounded, positive, value-neutral recourse to the empirical conditions of 'democracy' and the 'Rule of Law', then

[27] Hart, H.L.A., *The Concept of Law* (Clarendon Press, Oxford, 1961), 200.

we would happily agree that the moralisation of law, or the aspirations of legal idealism are quite superfluous. However, this cannot possibly be the case because, between the amorphous nature of democratic legitimation of government, on the one hand, and the unavoidable impasse of discretion and the open texture of rules, on the other, *all* decision-making which is not merely coin-tossing must be based on some conception of interests and of value. And if we were to undertake a moral analysis of the rational structure of democracy, and of law, that is, attempt to deduce some fundamental principles of normative rationality intrinsic to the practical structure of the democratic and legal enterprise, then we might come closer to understanding the nature of the principles which might serve as the boundaries of difficult or complex applications of discretion and interpretation. These boundaries would *simultaneously* appear *a priori* as the boundaries of the *legitimate* democratic or collective will.

Striving to achieve an understanding of the relationship between democratic and legal legitimacy is a pretty useful idea and perhaps should be the future of jurisprudence; but valorising some unspecified (or stipulating even a highly specific) conception of democracy over abstract 'morality' as the proper and superior ground of principle which should inform the interpretative process is so indeterminate as to be completely unhelpful.

5
Law as a Social Contract

It seems, in the light of the discussion in Chapter 4, that any view of society which values the individual and recognises the existence of basic rights, and certainly any view which subscribes to the notion of individual rights in a pluralist-democratic context, must eventually acknowledge a position which, from Rousseau and Kant to Habermas, broadly embraces the following ideas: (i) that moral aspirations can be achieved only by the formation of an artificial, yet publicly accessible, univocal standard of right (in the form of practical reasons or norms); (ii) that public institutions must be established and granted authority to overrule the unilateral moral or otherwise practical judgements and interpretations of right of individual citizens[1]; and (iii) that such institutions can be maintained only if these institutions can manifest their authority. This latter implies a demand for obedience and the necessary means to ensure such obedience. If this much is agreed, then we must in some way subscribe to what, as we noted in Chapter 2, Postema calls the Autonomy Thesis (AT). However, we must proceed carefully in the examination of the content and implications of such a conception, for it is from the analysis of law's alleged autonomy from morality that the issue of obligation will be settled.

Let us recall that Postema refers to three central components: the 'limited domain' thesis, the 'source' thesis and the 'preemption' thesis. And let us also recall that the fundamental impulse of the creation of an autonomous sphere of normativity is to respond to a general co-ordinatory problem in the pre-legal condition of society. We might, then, examine the logic of

---

[1] See our discussion in Chap. 2 *supra* at n. 9 and the corresponding text.

co-ordination in relation to the central elements of the AT, particularly in relation to the source thesis.

To achieve a better understanding of the role of the source thesis, we must direct our attention once again to the societal condition which, in general terms, gives rise to a need for it. The reasons for upholding the source thesis (as well as the pre-emption thesis) are to be found in the attempted solution to the problem of co-operation and co-ordination arising in relation to the pursuit (and achievement) of desired ends and projects in a social context. The problem is that individuals in society do not spontaneously work co-operatively for a common goal, nor is such co-operation necessarily guaranteed by prudence, morality or plain good will. There are many reasons why this is so: sheer contingency can cause us to oppose each other in particular ways. Where there is agreement on general aims there are often disparate and conflicting understandings of what these aims presuppose or imply in practical terms. Furthermore, the opacity and ambiguity of social interaction and, in a Hobbesian sense, cynicism concerning stated intentions of others often create a reluctance to co-operate or merely forbear. Why, after all, should I agree to co-ordinate my attempt to influence the structure of public life with others when I cannot be sure that their understanding of 'the good' and, hence, their ultimate intentions are not the same as mine? Why should I co-operate with others or, for their greater comfort, adopt more costly means to my own ends, if this militates against what I perceive to be my self-interest? More to the point, why should I act in this selfless manner when I cannot be sure that everyone else—or most people—will do the same? The 'source thesis' in conjunction with the 'pre-emption' thesis are steps to solving these problems.

The 'source-thesis' supplies us with a means of delimiting those reasons on which social co-ordination and co-operation are built. In other words, the source thesis helps to bring the 'limited domain' thesis to life. Those who argue in favour of the full (i.e. value-neutral) source thesis claim that the social problems which the source thesis is supposed to solve spring directly from moral (or otherwise evaluative) considerations, and that

114

therefore only a non-moral, non-evaluative criterion of recognition will do. If moral or other normative considerations are allowed to enter into the rule of recognition, then the original problem will simply be reproduced. The conclusion is that we need criteria which are public, empirically accessible and value-free. But this is not enough. In order to secure the efficiency of the limited domain thesis, we need to be sure, not only positively, that we have established a morality-free zone, but also negatively, in that practical reasons which do not spring from the authorised source do not enter the deliberative calculus of agents acting in a social setting. This is what is expressed by the pre-emption thesis. Only by blocking out the considerations that gave rise to the co-ordinatory and co-operative problems in the first place—for example, by making them unattractive through the idea of punishment or punitive monetary costs and so on—can we expect the source thesis to work. This is why Radbruch, we might recall, stresses the value of *Rechtssicherheit* (legal certainty) above all else. This understanding of the value and function of legal certainty is really the essence of the Autonomy Thesis.

However, as we noted in Chapter 2, we do not entirely endorse Radbruch's view that the value of certainty must, for the judge, take absolute priority. The reason for this is that we do not believe that it is rationally possible to make the *sacrificium intellectus* which is required by this view.[2] In our view, it is not possible nor is it desirable to insulate law hermetically from morality. Whilst appreciating the descriptive and prescriptive thrust of the idea of law's autonomy from the tangled struggle of political morality, and thus accepting the need for a form of 'artificial' reasoning appropriate to legality, we must attempt to qualify our agreement by arguing for a particular form of autonomy: what we shall refer to as *transparent* autonomy. The idea of transparency in public affairs is hardly novel; but we do attach a precise and, in our view, important meaning to it in the context of its relationship to legal authority and moral reason. For

[2] See Chap. 2 *supra*, pp. 35–41.

the moment we shall simply hint at what we have in mind by quoting the soldier and Leveller, John Lilburne. In what can now be seen as response in anticipation of Radbruch's claim that the duty of the judge is to be subservient to the law without regard to its justice, Lilburne writes[3]:

> there is in laws an equitable and a literall sense. . . . when there is certaine appearance or grounded suspicion, that the letter of the law shall be improved against the equitie of it . . . then the commander going against its equity, gives liberty to the commanded to refuse obedience to the letter: for the law taken abstract from its originall reason and end, is made a shell without a kernell, a shadow without a substance, and a body without a soul. It is the execution of laws according to their equity and reason, which (as I may say) is the spirit that gives life to Authority the Letter kills.

Lacking Lilburne's gifts we might say more prosaically that a *transparent* autonomy is a form of autonomy which allows the law's background considerations and justifications to shine through and illuminate the processes of interpretation and application. We shall return to what we see as the moral logic of this broad idea in the following chapter; but prior to this let us further consider the nature of the normative foundations of the AT.

In the form that Postema presents it, the AT has an extremely important consequence when expanded. That is, it necessarily leads us to consider the way in which the stock of settled norms alleged to be autonomous from the sphere of social and political morality is interpreted and applied. This introduces what we see as the pivotal issue in the explication and defence of the concept of autonomy. Postema says[4]:

> Defenders of the Autonomy thesis often locate it in a broader institutional conception of law, the key institution, for present purposes, being adjudicative (law-applying) institutions. The key idea is that

[3] See Lilburne, John (1645); 'England's Birthright Justified' in Haller W. (ed.) *Tracts on Liberty in the Puritan Revolution* (New York, Columbia University Press) pp. 259–260.

[4] Postema, Gerald, 'Law's Autonomy and Public Practical Reason' in George, R.P., *The Autonomy of Law: Essays on Legal Positivism* (Clarendon Press, Oxford, 1996), 79–119 at 93.

the law's solution to the pervasive problems of social co-operation essentially includes, but is not limited to, defining a set of norms that meet the conditions of the Autonomy Thesis; for these norms are authoritatively interpreted and applied, and the system of norms is maintained by adjudicative institutions.

He is, of course, right to say that the whole idea of a stock of settled norms implies a settled (i.e. institutionalised) procedure for application. This points to the need for a special group of authoritative personnel to carry out the task. Without such the idea of an autonomous stock of norms makes little or no sense. This institutionalisation, not just of autonomous norms, but of autonomous *interpretations* of norms, signals a crucial complexity in the idea of the AT: judges, says Postema, might *decide* the law, but they do not always reason *according* to law. He says[5]:

adjudicative institutions are authorized to settle issues left unsettled by the set of source-based legal norms available at any point in time. They are authorised to add to or alter the norms of law. Since, in such cases, by hypothesis, the existing legal considerations are silent, indeterminate, or in conflict, the courts' sett[l]ing of them is determined not by appeal to the law, but by appeals to considerations outside its limited domain.

The expansion of the AT to the *Institutionalised* Autonomy Thesis (IA Thesis) presents us with an immediate problem: we must now attempt to articulate the nature and scope of reasoning which inform the interpretative strategies of these adjudicative institutions in respect of the pre-emptive and co-ordinatory aims presupposed as practical justifications for the AT itself.

First, the very idea of the source thesis is in itself problematic. It may well be the case that establishing an unambiguous and empirical 'rule of recognition' prior to the process of interpreting the identified norm is as complex an issue as the problem of substantive interpretation of the norm itself, and if so, then the AT cannot be coherently argued.[6] But, this aside, if settled norms are

[5] *Ibid.*, 93.
[6] See e.g. Coleman, Jules, 'Authority and Reason' in George (n. 4 *supra*), 287–319 and also, importantly, MacCormick in the same volume, 163–93.

sometimes in need of interpretation *prior* to application—which hardly needs to be argued—and these interpretations appeal to reasons other than extant norms or reasons embedded in the normative stock of the limited domain, and especially if from this novel norms arise and override formerly settled norms, then the pre-emption thesis and the idea of autonomous law as consisting essentially in its significant isolation from political morality are threatened. Clearly, if interpretations of the norms—supposedly autonomous from political morality—are functions of evaluations from the very stock of political morality, then (*ex hypothesi* the AT) the logic of co-ordinatory advantage accruing, idealtypically, to practical reasoners in respect of stable expectations appears to be inconsistent in the absence of an auxiliary modification to its expanded corollary, the IA Thesis. In other words without an extremely complex theory of autonomous interpretation, the AT and IA Thesis do not achieve the completeness of a general autonomy *theory*. Referring to his comprehensive discussion of these fundamentals, Postema says[7]:

> in view of the problems we have already canvassed, we have no reason to assume that the Autonomy Thesis will survive the 'completion' of the theory. The best filling out of the theory may require that we qualify or even abandon the Autonomy Thesis. I suspect that the first casualty of this attempt to complete the theory will be the strategy of isolation lying at the heart of the Institutionalised Autonomy Theory. In its place we should look for a model which integrates arguments of political morality into proper legal argument and justification, starting from recognition of the reflectively self-critical character of legal practice.

We think this is correct; and in our view the first step towards achieving this integration is to acknowledge that there exists what we shall refer to as an *integrated continuum of practical reason*: from the prudential, to the moral, to the complexity of the political, and from political authority to the 'autonomy' of legality. In other words we must seek to grasp a connection between the fundamental phenomenological stages of practical reason

[7] Postema (n. 4 *supra*), 111.

through to its institutionalised, pre-emptive applications. We might note that at no point need we necessarily speak of 'law' or even 'morality', these being merely shorthand terms for particular conditions, implications, applications and contextualisations of the dialectic of the practical. Refraining from so doing at least helps to remind us that there is—or might be—a continuum of practical reason, and so render the assertion of a qualitative discontinuity within it much less plausible.

This practical continuum can be more clearly illustrated if we move to a simple comparative discussion of classical models of the social contract which, we will suggest, might usefully be seen as attempts to complete (or avoid) the missing link in the IA *Theory*. The AT and the IA Thesis clearly presuppose a problem-solving move from the 'pre-legal' to the 'legal' and the subsequent problem of determining the nature and bounds of authority and obligation consistent with the attempt to solve the problem giving rise to the move. We think that we can convincingly encompass all possible proponents of the initial Autonomy Thesis (AT) in this shift by remaining, at least at this stage of the discussion, agnostic as to the moral condition of the notionally pre-positive, pre-legal condition, and neutral in respect of the mode of practical justification adduced to explain or rationally reconstruct the move from moral diversity (or what might be called a 'state of nature') to autonomy (i.e. 'civil society' or, as Unger might say, 'legal order'). We are merely required to presuppose that there exists a *plausible* case for the institutionalisation of an autonomous normativity to effect the move from an unregulated and uncertain state of affairs to a stable societal condition.

The IA Theory as a Social Contract

The perspective of law as a legitimate political strategy (the *complete* IA Theory) or what we will argue is, in effect, a social contract theory, moves through four stages in the attempt to trace the logic of social incorporation, that is, the practical logic of the initial social compact from the condition of a state of nature to the institutionalised processes of legitimation in advanced

119

society. Before discussing these stages in order to reveal our central point, let us sketch three conveniently simple models of justificatory practical reason leading to the kind of normative incorporation envisaged by the AT. We will refer to them purely for convenience as: 'prudential' (e.g. more or less Hobbes); 'quasi-moral' (Aquinas, Finnis and perhaps, it seems, more or less Hart, MacCormick and Raz); and 'moral' (e.g. more or less Locke).

Prudential Models

Let us imagine, with Hobbes, that the idea of right is non-existent in the pre-legal state. Prudence and self-preservation alone get us into the situation where we must seek peace, and this requires an incarnation of autonomous right: a sovereign. The sovereign's word is final, and obedience (obligation) is prudentially necessary and justified as our part of the compact of the voluntary surrender of natural freedom for protection and assurance of performance of mutual covenants. Broadly speaking, sovereign authority is limited only in relation to the failure to protect.[8] Let us note that we could update this moral scepticism to a full blown 'scientific' ethical non-cognitivism or a Weberian or Kelsenian positivism. Here value conflict—plurality—requires a settled procedural format for co-ordinatory and dispute-resolutionary purposes and the production of 'valid' autonomous norms.

Quasi-moral Models

Finnis, like Aquinas, holds that underpinning the unfathomable and irreconcilable diversity of moral opinion and conceptions of the good, there are natural laws (as opposed to strictly prudential maxims) discoverable by reason; these point us to basic goods which a rational being should seek.[9] A co-ordinated society based on posited law is one of them, but the positive law is so far removed in contextual complexity from the natural prin-

[8] Hobbes, Thomas, *Leviathan* (C.B. McPherson (ed.), London, Pelican, 1968) chap. 21, 114.

[9] See Finnis, John, *Natural Law and Natural Rights* (Clarendon Press, Oxford, 1980), 59ff.

ciples, and ranges over so many—as he says—'incommensurable' values,[10] that the Natural Law must be seen as too indeterminate an influence to supply a plausible and intersubjectively workable basis for validating the vast majority of interpretations and applications required of the positive law. The justificatory reasoning of positive law is thus to be seen as *qualitatively discontinuous* with morality, and the basis of obligations arising is to be referred not to morality, but to the logic of positive normativity (autonomy) itself.

Moral Models

Against this (as might be ideal-typically reconstructed in, e.g., Locke[11]) the general principles of moral right, duty and property are held to exist in the state of nature, but application of right and assertion of right and redress of wrongs spring from fallible unilateral (individually reasoned) and thus unpredictable judgements. Moral reason tells us that right and just freedoms can be realised only when institutionalised in civil society. We are of right duty bound (i.e. practical reason requires us) to enrol and coerce others into civil society. A law-giver or sovereign body is established, but its laws are valid only if posited consistently within the limits of the fundamental moral rationale which gave rise to need of them. The sovereign's word, however, other than in profoundly pathological circumstances, must be generally obeyed, because strident unilateral debate about or assertion of the moral conditions of the validity of law reproduces the problem that law was intended to solve.

State of Nature to Rule of Law: 4 Stages

What seems helpful, then, is to suggest a broad taxonomy of views between:

> (1) those who maintain that there are many moral opinions but no moral truths in the original position, and advocate autonomous law as a solution. Thus we might include, as

[10] See *ibid.*, 92; also our discussion of this issue in Chap. 6 *infra*.

[11] Locke, John, *The Second Treatise on Government* (Gough J.W. (ed.), Basil Blackwell, Oxford, 1946).

noted, Hobbes, Weber or Kelsen, i.e. a *procedural* (or 'pedi-gree' or 'source' based) positivism;

(2) those who conceive of the validity of natural laws (objec-tive values) in a state of nature, believe that they should be followed as far as possible, yet, *a priori*, regard them as effec-tively indeterminate in informing interpretation and adjudica-tion and supplying the justification for obedience at any significant level of societal complexity;

(3) those who take the view that morality exists in the state of nature and implies and justifies the institutionalisation of right in civil society, that the principles of this pre-legal morality ought to inform legal reason in respect of its procedural and substantive tasks of positing, interpreting and applying laws and thus provide the moral justification for its claims to authority and the account of legal obligation. The difference between (2) and (3) then, is an *a priori* divergence of view over the issue of whether practical reason, post-incorporation—i.e. *post* AT—differs in kind or merely in degree from practical reason at the *pre*-incorporation—i.e. *pre*-AT stage. (3) appears to be the best bet for a candidate for a Natural Law or Legal Idealist account of the legal enterprise whereas (1) appears to deny the link to morality altogether, but yet appears to be dis-tinct from (2). Let us pursue in more detail the logic of the move from diversity, or the state of nature, to incorporation (or autonomy or 'law') in civil society.

We are indebted to the real, textual John Locke (who in turn is indebted to many before him[12]) for alerting us to the idea of the dual stages of incorporation by introducing the idea of trusteeship (rather than the surrender) of power or authority subsequent to the compact of incorporation. This serves to inform our thinking about the limits of government and the basic rights and real interests of individuals. This two stage process appears to have the advantage over the 'prudential' (schematically Hobbesian) argument (1) in allowing, abstractly

[12] See Locke, John, *The Second Treatise on Government* (Gough J.W. (ed.), Basil Blackwell, Oxford, 1946), and Gough's introductory remarks in this regard.

and in terms of a theoretical reconstruction, the practically reasonable party to the contract to retain—*vis-à-vis* basic rights and interests—some control and input into the *pre-emptive* programme of exclusionary reasons established by the authorities empowered by the contract. The 'Lockean' strategy (3), because of this reference to the caveat of fundamental and motivating rights and interests, we have called the 'moral' strategy. The 'moral' strategy, however, has in a sense a tendency to reproduce the difficulties which made the strategy of incorporation—or AT—a practically reasonable manœuvre in the first place. That is, the idea of trusteeship (explicit in Locke) makes the idea of moral justifications of rights and real interests central to the question of the validity of the laws. If this occurs, the reasons for the purposes of legislation, the scope of the legislation and the interpretation of the laws rests, ideal-typically, on the identification of these rights and (real) interests. This can but result in moral debate; no doubt presented ostensibly in a philosophical and universalist fashion, but possibly underpinned by all manner of sectional and strategic motives.

The Hobbesian or 'Prudential' solution (1) (conveniently simplified) is to short-circuit this unwelcome possibility by using the very logic which entails these potential ramifications as the justification for a once-and-for-all 'allocation of the say' to an absolute sovereign.[13] However, even accepting without demur that some form of incorporation and normative predictability is desirable, it is by no means self-evident, in terms of the logic of bare prudence, that this absolutism should appear as an attractive strategy.

The notional Lockean ('moral') solution (3) arising from these misgivings is to determine the nature and extent of the relevant rights and interests *a priori* as a pre-determined check on the essential and primary power of political authority. In other words, the logic which informs positive application of the law in civil society must be made consistent with the moral purposes for which an incorporated and autonomous sphere was invented

---

[13] See n. 8 *supra*.

and institutionalised in the first place. The optimistic idea put
forward in this model is that these allegedly universal purposes
are identifiable and thus unproblematic, and unlikely to foment
dispute if we take the precaution of having them clearly written
into the logic of incorporation and, thence, into the conditions
of the trusteeship *ab initio*. The apparent dichotomy between (1)
and (3) (broadly, Hobbes and Locke) established by this distinction, however, is not as clear-cut as it might appear. In fact,
brief reflection upon it illustrates a dialectical third stage of what
is fast becoming a caricatured example of the idea of 'the negation of the negation'. That is, moral conflict, normative uncertainty and the vulnerability of rights and interests in the state of
nature bring forth the logic of autonomy as expressed in the
basic version of AT; yet the need to constrain and prefigure the
autonomous forces of law created and set in motion leads us to
reflect upon the immanent principles and boundaries of laws
protective of, and conducive to, the flourishing of basic rights
and real interests *which first brought it into being.*

Now, switching momentarily to the framework of the AT, in
terms of the problematic 'completion' of the IA Theory we have
a genuine choice between our 'Prudential' (Hobbesian), and
'Moral' (Lockean) models, only if at least one of them remains
consistent with at least stages (i) and (ii) of the process from
state of nature to civil society—i.e. effectively the expression of
the AT, that is (i) acknowledgement of the intolerable condition
of pre-legality, and (ii) a subsequent act of incorporation; stage
(iii)—the strategy of autonomy—remaining to be designed on
the basis of our choices at this stage. The point is that, if we opt
for a Lockean-style limitation of the sovereignty of autonomous
law, we must conceive of its validity in terms of a system of
practical reasoning and justification which moves to applicative
conclusions (positive laws) from premises which express
propositions which either claim universal validity for certain categorical imperatives or purport to identify certain intrinsic goods
which imply these categorical imperatives: i.e. imply the ethical
first principles which ground the practical reasonableness of
incorporation. The problem is that even if these first principles
124

are not only true, and not only plausibly and demonstrably true, but generally accepted as such, the unavoidable generality of these principles can but admit of a range of plausible and reasonable (not to mention perverse and unreasonable—but not, we would argue, within any logically consistent scheme of practical reason, *incommensurable*) options at the point of their interpretation and application in highly complex and imperfectly understood historical circumstances. This problem is compounded if it is sometimes the case that the question of the cognitive apprehension of the nature or the relevance of the 'factual' circumstances is somehow dependent upon the interpretation of the principles in question. Unfortunately, it seems highly likely that this is indeed the situation in which we find ourselves in relation to the issue of authority founded upon, and limited by, ethical or moral or 'natural law' first principles.

So, from our political-strategic (social contract) perspective, we have now considered four stages of the dialectic: (i) acknowledgement of the unacceptable condition (for individuals and social sub-groups) of a pre-legal state of nature; (ii) the move to some form of incorporation in civil society; (iii) establishment of the terms and principles of the trusteeship (or sovereignty) of the powers resulting from incorporation, and finally (iv) the problem of settling the criteria of valid interpretation and application of positive law in relation to the principles so established. Thus even if we accept the force of reasoning in stages (i) (ii) and (iii), stage (iv) throws us back—admittedly on a different plane—to the issue of plurality and disagreement: the situation which Hobbes anticipates so swiftly and expresses so clearly at stage (iii) of his (actual) argument.[14] In the event of no further

[14] Hobbes says:

'All Laws written, and unwritten, have need of Interpretation. The unwritten Law of Nature, though it be easy to such, as without partiality, and passion, make use of their naturall reason, and therefore leave the violators thereof without excuse; yet considering there be few, perhaps none, that in some cases are not blinded by self love, or some other passion, it is now become of all Laws the most obscure; and has consequently the greatest need of able Interpreters'—Hobbes (n. 8 *supra*), 322.

refinement to the interpretative process at stage (iv), it seems that the strategic (Hobbesian/Lockean) dichotomy collapses. We either have, straight off, the 'Prudential' (Hobbesian) maxim: 'law is that which the sovereign decrees to be law', or we postpone this absolutist conclusion to a later stage. That is, we hold to a 'Moral' logic to move us through stages (i) (ii) and (iii) before *then* adopting a Hobbesian strategy for finalising dispute between (hypothetically) all possible and (in practice) all actual claims to interpretation of the terms and principles of trusteeship or sovereignty at stage (iv).

This latter produces a contradiction either way. We cannot (a) coherently rely on a strategy which we admit to be so indeterminate as to reproduce the moral dissonance which (as Postema anticipates in the problem of developing the IA Theory as a function of the AT) motivated the move from stage (i) to stage (ii) in the first place; and (b), in countering this tendency to instability; abandon to a Hobbesian absolutism the genetic principles of moral right upon which we rely for the practical justification of the initial move to incorporation. If we do, we expose our primary reasonings as merely wistful musings which might, admittedly, add rhetorical respectability to the (actually) uncontrollable and possibly interest-inimical authority we seek to institutionalise and unleash. This contradiction is reproduced, *a fortiori* and *ex hypothesi*, by the even more indeterminate 'quasi-moral' model (2) of the argument to incorporation or AT. Thus, unless we settle for the 'prudential' (absolutist) strategy, we are forced to reconsider the problem of how we might preserve the determinate moral force of the principles which characterise the practical rationale of the decision to move to incorporation. In other words, we must contemplate how we might effect theoretical closure of the IA Theory, or, alternatively, contemplate abandoning altogether the AT which, since the unavoidable introduction of the idea of *institutionalised* interpretations and applications of norms (i.e., the IA *Thesis*) has been extremely troublesome.

We must, then, countenance the possibility of developing a criterion which will at least allow us to identify and distinguish *plausible and reasonable* interpretations and applications of the natural or moral first principles which inform our positive law, from the *de facto* possible, but rationally perverse or unfounded, claims and perspectives which might arise. Unless we admit this possibility we do indeed subvert—in fact deny—the intelligibility of the 'moral' approach. This is not a moral argument in itself; it is a matter of simple logical form: even Hobbes admits that the prudence of protection does not cohere with contracting into obedience to one who refuses or fails to protect. But neither, we might add, does this principle of naked self-interest in preserving ourselves from harm escape from the problems which might arise in establishing a criterion which would allow us plausibly and reasonably to ascertain—that is, *interpret*—just what constitutes the absence of protection.

The Continuity of Practical Reason

The logic of autonomy in stage (iii) from any perspective must then contain sufficient provision for the identification of a finite range of possibly acceptable claims to reasonable interpretations of the foundational principles. This does not solve the problem of indeterminacy completely, but formally it would deliver it into a bounded sphere of 'reasonable' as opposed to 'unreasonable' options. To say that this limitation is not possible within the sphere of autonomous law in civil society is to say that a theory of institutionalised practical reasoning is not possible; because if this much is not possible, neither is it possible to argue for a move from the 'state of nature' in the first place, there being, hypothetically, just as many possible *de facto* expressions of objection to the practical reasonableness of it (all of 'equal' weight) as there might be in favour of it. If, however, we admit that we might move from the 'state of nature' to civil society, to institutionalised, autonomous, positive law on the basis of practical reason which appeals to some generalisable conception of fundamental human interests, we must admit *ex hypothesi* that the principle in question must at least furnish a criterion to enable us to determine that some conceptions of the implications of practical reason are indeed *reasonable*, and that some are not. Our first aspiration, therefore, is to develop a filter process whereby only 'reasonable' examples of the employment of practical reason are considered as possible candidates for authoritative interpretation.

Following this, the sensitive problem arising will be the issue of a conflicting plurality of interests within the range of rational options—a range so extensive that intersubjective agreement on the eligibility of the candidate options might be in short supply. For, admittedly, we might agree that a range of interpretations of right were, *prima facie*, rationally on a par—yet subsequently acknowledge that, as an indirect or coincidental upshot of the application of one particular view, certain constituencies of interests would benefit, or suffer loss or disadvantage, absolutely or relatively in relation to others. It seems that in these circumstances the best we could possibly do is develop a refinement which might further narrow the range of possible options *vis-à-vis* interests, by searching for integrally consistent criteria which could grade the general relative weight of interests involved in the adjudicative process.[15] If this is the best we can do there is little point in expecting more of moral reasoning in relation to the justification of positive law. In the next and final chapter, we will try to explain what is meant by a public and accountable attempt 'to do our best' in this regard. Thus we accept the thesis of law's autonomy from morality only in the sense that this autonomy must be a *transparent* attempt to preserve the moral impulse which demands its autonomous operation.

[15] We discuss this important strategy in some detail in relation to Gewirth's hierarchy of dispositional features of agency in Chap. 6.

6
The Elements of Transparent Autonomy

We enter a concluding phase by saying that we are confident that if there is enough practical rationality to get us into the Autonomy Thesis, there ought to be enough to get us out of it. Getting out of it *rationally* means completing the Autonomy *Theory* by demonstrating the logical possibility of a stable and general theory of interpretation and application of institutionalised norms. But let us not assume that this is merely a problem of adjudication. This familar focal point of jurisprudential debate arises simply because jurisprudence tends to enter the debate *inside* law and move linearly to the end process of application. But, as we saw in our discussion of morality and democracy in Chapter 4, if we begin instead from the perspective of political philosophy, we must see law as a necessary mechanism, both procedurally and substantively, for the institutionalisation of will-formation and, in this case, the focus shifts to the other pole of the analysis, i.e. the political creation of conditions for constitutionally legitimate government. So, the *reactive* problem of legal interpretation and application has its *proactive* counterpart in the problem of conceptualising the basis for what constitutes valid law-*making*.[1] This problem can be articulated only by recourse to the moral-philosophical, sociological and economic grounds for the notion of the legitimacy of political authority. Ideas such as 'Sovereign', 'State', the transformation

[1] A clear discussion of this issue of continuity in the context of the morality of legal positivism is to be found in John Gardner's review of Tom Campbell's *The Legal Theory of Ethical Positivism* (Dartmouth, Aldershot, 1996) in (1998) 9 *KCLJ* 180.

of a 'multitude' into a 'People', a separation of powers, the idea of representation, 'critical' public opinion and so on—all indispensable notions—point towards the logical priority of a moral criterion. Familiar jurisprudential problems of interpretation and application have been the occasion for the discussion and argument presented so far in this book, but we hope that we have made more than a perfunctory case for the importance of locating legal theory within a bigger picture. In the light of this let us attend to the details of the way a precise conception of natural moral reason might give rise to, and interact with, legal form.

In Chapters 2 and 5 we suggested that 'natural' morality and 'artificial' reasoning formed two halves of an integrated whole of legal reasoning. Positivism, broadly conceived, appeared to prioritise the formal values of predictability and certainty over substantial moral concerns, and this, we suggested, was a mistaken approach to the problem. Rather, we have promoted the view that legal validity arises from an assiduous attempt to promulgate and apply norms in a framework of reasoning that remains morally integral with practically rational responses to regulatory and co-ordinatory problems within a society. Legal validity is the condition to which rule-makers and adjudicators must singularly aspire in the attempt to provide an authoritative and reasonable justification for compliance. In other words, a norm is legally valid when it can be said that such a norm ought to be applied and obeyed.

In the last part of Chapter 2 we argued that what is characteristic of law is the setting up of a system of artificial reasoning based on autonomous authoritative principles. By locking the representatives of the state (governmental officials, judges etc.) on to such a system, it becomes possible to channel the reasoning of these representatives and, hence, possible to develop a stable control of the vagaries and limitations of individual human reasoning. The idea behind such a system of artificial reasoning is, of course, that it allows for predictability and accountability. An ordering of this kind makes it difficult for the representatives of the state to take advantage of the system by promoting their own private interests or their own personal perception of what

130

is morally right or wrong. A legal formalism, therefore, appears to be a *sine qua non* of the system prior to any substantive considerations. But we must remember that the very idea of legal validity arises first from the acknowledgment of the need to respond to substantive and inherent moral conflict in society. It is this condition that forces us to accept the optimally reasonable practical insight into the need to establish and develop an 'artificial' or formal edifice through the *institutionalisation* of autonomous normativity. We must not, then, be seduced by the convenience of a one-dimensional conception of legal validity which relates to legal *form* alone and the simple pragmatics of legal certainty. For this produces the thin gruel of legal validity 'in the technical sense'.[2] Legal form, we argued, is inherently moral. Let us briefly consider what it entails.

Categories, Procedures and Rules

The most important aspects of legal form comprise the concern for (a) categories, (b) procedure, and (c) rules. Concerning (a), we can say that legal formalism consists of the fitting of actions and actors into certain legally constructed categories. Actions and actors are abstracted from their natural social settings and 'filed' in pre-defined, often rigid, legal categories. The categories in turn are related to legal norms as the basic elements in defining prohibited/permitted action. Procedure (b) relates to an emphasis on the need to make legal statements, judgments and activities adhere to certain linguistic, temporal and official forms of expression and development. This concern is related to the pragmatic (as opposed to moral) dimension of authority, that is, the requirement of the law's capacity to effect a terminus of argument or dispute. If legal decisions were open to endless question on substantive grounds, the law would not be able to serve the purpose of making an end to dispute. Procedural rules also help to make the legal system more efficient in simple terms of labour, time and effort. Concerning (c), a rule is the

[2] See Chap. 2 *supra*, pp. 42–50.

statement of a norm; and we can say that legal formalism consists of a concern for making legal judgments accord with stable, explicit and public procedural norms. Legal judgments must be made on the basis of rules so conceived, not simply on the basis of what a judge might think is desirable. Thus the concern for rules, as Lon Fuller comprehensively explains, is really a concern for the idea of an 'inner morality' of law: equality, generality and predictability inherent in the general idea of the Rule of Law.[3] In a state where the Rule of Law applies, the law not only prescribes, in terms of positive rules, how people ought to behave under certain factual conditions, it is simultaneously the basis on which people who hold authority in the state make official decisions.

Formalistic Interpretation: Facts and Norms

This problem is somewhat more complex. Interpretation occurs at both the factual and normative stages of reasoning in the law. At the factual stage, interpretation becomes relevant and important because, for the purposes of making legal judgments, lawyers are not so much interested in facts as they are in *statements of facts*. That is, the same facts can be presented in various ways, and it is the nature of the presentation which is important, not the facts themselves. Facts, it is said, are facts; but in relation to the making of legal judgments, facts are stated with a view to making a decision. When presenting the facts, some details (which are also facts) are left out, while other details are emphasised. This creates a particular view of a situation for legal purposes. This shaping of reality, which takes place in the judicial process, is necessary for the legal system to function. Only by distinguishing the relevant from the irrelevant

---

[3] See Fuller, Lon. L., *The Morality of Law* (New Haven, Yale University Press, 1964). Other ways of conceptualising the nature of legal formalism can be found in Weinrib, Ernest J. (1996), *Why Legal Formalism?* and Raz, Joseph (1996), *Formalism and the Rule of Law*, both in George, R.P. (ed.), *Natural Law Theory* (Clarendon Press, Oxford, 1992).

facts is it possible to fit or 'file' the facts in a form in which it is possible to process them within the system in question.

Legal norms rely on factual categories, in that every norm has an area of application, but these factual categories are artificial in the sense that they are created by the law, and do not follow natural patterns. The law constructs an ordered reality in which its constituent norms can be applied. This is not unusual. All social practices are in some way structured; the legal system relies on an ordering and structuring of reality, the categories of which are sometimes, perhaps often, different from the categories used in other social spheres. We might say that law's reality in this sense is autonomous from social reality outside its limited domain.[4] When making legal judgments, therefore, the construction of reality is crucial, because it informs, conditions and predisposes ensuing evaluation, selection and application of what are considered appropriate normative responses. Thus even though law's construction of reality is autonomous and formalistic, it is also normative and value-laden. But how do we measure whether the legal form chosen is the right one? This is a simple question with a complex answer. But we have at least said enought to know that this evaluation must not be based on shifting and unpredictable personal preferences. The formal answer is that it should be based on a coherent and accessible scheme of practical rationality capable of incorporating both the substantive and procedural aspects of the problem of legitimacy. We shall revisit this general claim in more detail presently.

At the next stage of interpretation, the question relates to what kind of action the legal rule prescribes. This is a question of defining the normative content of the rule. Here there is an interplay between legal formalism and moral interpretation. Legal formalism shows itself in the reliance on legal *sources* and in the canons of legal interpretation. One of the most basic assumptions of legal systems (and legal theory) is that rules, to be legal, must be created by a recognised institution. This, then, is the starting point: a set of rules which satisfy a certain criterion of

[4] Comparative law studies, of course, show us that different legal systems may work with different categories.

'recognition'. But in order to specify the normative content, one must not only identify the 'rule' *qua* the locus of appropriate legal materials; one must interpret first the normative scope of those materials and then, following a complex and (in practice) always contentious set of judgements about what this is, isolate the rule.[5] Upon this impressive achievement the familiar problem of judicial interpretation now takes place. In relation to this stage of procedure, legal doctrine has developed certain familiar canons of interpretation.[6] But despite their existence, we are often left unedified in relation to the interpretive problem. There are several reasons why this is so.

First, the canons of interpretation are themselves in need of interpretation. How does one, for example, decide on the intentions of Parliament? Or how does one distinguish the plain meaning from the not-so-plain meaning. Obviously, an interpretation which is guided primarily by a strict reading of the wording of the statute might lead to a different result from an interpretation which gives effect to the intention of Parliament. Thus the outcome of the interpretive process depends on the canon chosen. In both (or any) cases one has to presuppose a normative framework within which the canons operate. Thus the real problem becomes one of deciding the criteria according to which one chooses the canon of interpretation. Professionally, an advocate arguing a case for one of his clients will argue on the basis of the canon which best suits his perception of the client's interests. In so far as legal institutions are *fora* for dispute resolution, parties to the dispute can pick and choose among the formally recognised canons of interpretation. The strategic manipulation of these formally recognised canons is what gives legal practice its argumentative character. But at some point, one

---

[5] An excellent discussion of this in relation to Dworkin and Hart's views is to be found in Beyleveld, Deryck, and Brownsword, Roger, *Law as a Moral Judgment* (Sweet and Maxwell, London, 1986), 413–23.

[6] See, conveniently and for example, the indispensable collection of writings from Cardozo, MacCormick, Levi, etc., in Freeman, M.A. (ed.), *Lloyd's Introduction to Jurisprudence* (6th edn., Sweet and Maxwell, London, 1994), chap. 15.

has to settle for one interpretation over another, and at this point it is no longer enough simply to be a master in manipulating the interpretation to fit this or that interest. At the point of authorised decision making in law, the person responsible for making the decision is responsible for making the *right* decision. The basic question for anyone in such a position then becomes, or rather returns to, the following: by what standard do I measure whether the legal form chosen is the right one? Just as in relation to the *factual* stage of interpretation, it is obvious that one cannot make such a decision on the basis of adhering only to 'the law', for, formalistically speaking, the dispute in question and the issue of what constitutes an appropriate response to it depend precisely on the question of what 'the law' prescribes. The idea of legal form and of procedure is an intrinsically moral notion—not merely an adjunct to, or a substitute for, moral reasoning. There is an unfriendly, if not an entirely vicious, air of circularity to this problem. An understanding of moral reasoning is, then, logically prior to our understanding of legal form, and we might see this as a point of departure in articulating the idea of a 'transparent autonomy'. One thing seems clear: if morality offers us no basis for developing decision-making criteria in substantive matters, we should not assume that we might thus seek a basis for authoritative decision making in pure formalism; for formalism is not 'pure' in this respect.

Finnis: Legal Authority and Moral Incommensurability

Our position throughout has been that the positivist option in general, or the possibility of a non-moral conception of legal authority and, hence, legal validity, rests upon a denial of a workable continuum of practical reason. Let us note that this issue is not primarily a jurisprudential matter but, rather, an issue in moral epistemology. The problem has two stages: (i) does prudential reason necessarily imply moral reason, and (ii) if so, can moral reason survive the process of institutionalisation from its natural state to a controllable and stable, if artificial and formalised, scheme of public practical reasoning. Those who might respond negatively to the inquiry in (i) will not be motivated to concern themselves with the issue raised in (ii). The epistemologically sceptical position—i.e. the negative response to (i)—reduces our options quite dramatically and forces us to conceptualise legal authority on the basis of what we referred to in Chapter 1 as a concept of 'normatively enhanced prudence'.[7] Only a non-cognitivist prejudice would prevent us, *prima facie*, from assuming that there is at least as much potential merit in the alternative position and, thus, let us consider the problem in (ii) on the basis of affirming the claim in (i).

Very generally, the acceptance of the move in (i) leads us to the idea of the rationality of acting in the interests of others on the basis of premisses which demonstrate the rationality of acting in our own interest. This kind of reasoning gives rise to the idea of rights and duties, and in turn gives us a perspective on the nature of institutionalised obligations which might arise given the task of enforcing or encouraging social acknowledgment of the consequences of practical reason in general, and prudence in particular. We suggested that 'the instrumental', 'the prudential', 'the moral' and 'the legal' formed a continuum subsumed by the general category of 'the practical'. The nature of the relationship between the legal and the moral *vis-`a-vis* valid or rationally authoritative reasoning thus depends upon these two crucial moments of analysis: the claim that prudential reason *does* necessarily imply moral reason; and, given that this is a valid inference, the possibility of the application of moral reason in the public context of enforceable prescription.

We can show how important this is by contrasting two views. The first, argued by Finnis, is one which accepts the validity of the move from prudential to moral reason, but declares morality to be *unworkable* as a basis for legal authority by virtue of the 'incommensurability of values'. Against this we will argue that the continuum of practical reason locates law as part of the moral continuum and that valid legal reasoning leading to

[7] See Chap. 1, *supra*, n. 28.

authoritative decisons can and must take place within a moral framework. We will try to show that it makes no sense to suggest that moral reason leads us to establish legal authority, but that, once established, the idea of 'authority' is to be seen as logically detached from the moral-practical basis of justification for the employment of such authority.

What, then, does John Finnis mean when he tells us that morality consist of incommensurable values? An illuminating route into his thinking in this regard is provided by examining his debate with Joseph Raz on the issue of the nature of obligation.[8] Raz, famously, denies the existence of a general obligation under law, arguing correctly, but unusually for a legal positivist, that obligation is an exclusively moral matter. Finnis argues that there are objective moral fundamentals, but that these do not admit of indirect application because of the incommensurability of values. He maintains, however, that moral fundamentals show us that, as practical reasoners, we must pursue the good, and that law (or 'authority') is a necessary means to the pursuit of the good.

Finnis, in *Natural Law and Natural Rights*, holds that the practically reasonable person must presuppose or instantiate a structure of basic goods in all their reasoning.[9] The practically reasonable life, for Finnis, is a pursuit of the good, but this takes many forms and no one form can be regarded as better or more worthwhile than any other. The basic goods, for Finnis, are all equally valuable; all equally fundamental. It is to this fact (leading to the 'intransitivity' of goods) which, in a brilliant critique of what he calls 'emaciated conceptions of practical reason', he points as the ground of the failure of 'Game Theory', 'Social

[8] See, importantly, Raz, Joseph, 'The Obligation to Obey: Revision and Tradition' (1984), *Notre Dame Journal of Law, Ethics and Public Policy* 141–55; Finnis, John, 'The Authority of Law in the Predicament of Contemporary Social Theory (*ibid.*), 115–37. A critical discussion is to be found in Batnitzky, Leora, 'A Seamless Web? John Finnis and Joseph Raz on the Obligation to Obey the Law' (1995) 15, *Oxford Journal of Legal Studies*, 153–77.

[9] For a detailed analysis see Toddington, Stuart, *Rationality, Social Action and Moral Judgment* (Edinburgh University Press, Edinburgh,1993), chap. 6.

Choice Theory', Benthamite Utilitarianism and Rawls's idea of the Original Position, to provide a useful model of rational action.[10] His point, and the view we were anxious to support in our opening chapter, is that practical reason takes us beyond prudence conceived as mere self-interest. According to Finnis, however, it leads to a complex matrix of moral goods in which no hierarchy of value is to be found. This, in essence, is what he means by the incommensurability of values. Law, for Finnis, is authoritative because it is a universally valid precept of practical reason that some type of 'authority' is required in order to create the conditions under which the complex and multi-dimensional idea of the good might be pursued. But this 'authority' cannot claim a moral omniscience to judge and rank the many and various forms this pursuit might take. Thus, in Finnis, the idea of practical reason begins with instrumentality and prudence, leads us beyond 'emaciated' self-interest to the notion of the good, demonstrates the necessity of the institutionalisation of practical reasoning and right in the form of law, but then seems to cast us adrift (apart from 'the most basic categories of moral right'[11]) in regard to the direction we then must take. Values are incommensurable. We are left with a detached and disembodied idea of authority—authority which, however, says Finnis, creates a general obligation to obey the law *because law is a necessary means* to the pursuit of (incommensurable) goods. Individuals, then, should realise that law or legal authority is in itself a good to be valued. It is a good[12]:

> indiscernible in the emaciated model of practical reasonableness; the good of a fair method of relating burdens to benefit, and persons to persons, over an immensely complex and lasting but shifting set of persons and their aspirations and transactions. Nothing other than legal order can promise such a method.

[10] See Finnis (n. 8 *supra*), 123–7.

[11] See Finnis, John, 'The Truth in Legal Positivism' and George's reiteration of this point in George, R.P. (ed.), *The Autonomy of Law* (Clarendon Press, Oxford, 1996).

[12] Finnis, n. 8 *supra*, 137.

We agree that nothing other than legal order can fulfill these aspirations; but are these aspirations consistent with the thesis of moral incommensurability? Let us see how this view interacts with Dworkin's insistence to the contrary that law's continuing authority relies on finding some determinate or 'right' answers to moral questions.

Finnis and Dworkin

John Finnis criticises Dworkin's suggestions as to how we might optimally approach problems of reasoning in hard cases on the point that the values which are central to morality and law in such cases are incommensurable.[13] If it were indeed possible to settle such cases, Finnis argues, these cases would not be hard cases. If it were possible to show that one answer to the legal problem at hand was rationally preferable to any other answer, then there would be no rational alternatives to the solution of the case and, hence, it would be an 'easy' case.[14] Let us say a few words in defence of Dworkin. Finnis's basic characterisation of morality, with which we can agree, is as follows[15]:

> Moral thought is simply rational thought at full stretch, integrating emotions and feelings, but undeflected by them . . . The fundamental principle of moral thought is simply the demand to be fully rational: in so far as it is in your power, allow nothing but the basic reasons for action to shape your practical thinking as you find, develop, and use your opportunities to pursue human flourishing through your chosen actions. Be entirely reasonable.

The problem that arises, of course, is what does it mean to be fully rational? What is human flourishing? And what does it mean to be entirely reasonable? These questions are identical to the questions that bring about the need for an institutionalisation of public practical reasoning in the form that we associate

[13] Finnis, John, 'Natural Law and Legal Reasoning' in George, R.P., *Natural Law* (Clarendon Press, Oxford, 1981), 134–57.

[14] *Ibid.*, 143–8.

[15] *Ibid.*, 136–7 (original emphasis).

with law. In such a system some people are granted authority to settle questions of what morality in complex situations requires. The idea, or the ideology, of a division of labour between a legislature which makes general rules (indirect moral norms) and a judicary which applies them emerges. The development of these and other institutions leads to an even higher societal complexity, and the creation of what we have called an 'artificial' (practical) reasoning, where the original moral problems seem to dissolve themselves in political discussions and legal technicalities. That this is true is displayed precisely in the so called 'hard' legal cases where answers to what is *legally* right are difficult and controversial because the moral backdrop to the case is problematic.

When making decisions in law, Dworkin argues, one must draw on two separate strings of reason. The first one is to a large extent empirical and is called the dimension of 'fit'. This string of legal reasoning requires that decisions in law must be in conformity with the existing legal material. The other is called the dimension of 'justification'. This string of legal reasoning requires that decisions in law must be morally sound. By relying on this scheme of reasoning, Dworkin believes that it is possible to find right answers to all legal cases, including the hard ones. The key to the right decision is to find the right balance between the two dimensions of legal reasoning, and this balancing act Dworkin describes by the use of the metaphor of preserving the narrative integrity of a chain novel.[16] The right answer to a case is one in which the *full scope* of the existing legal material is first *identified*[17] and then interpreted in a way which renders the decision as morally sound as possible. We might say that the decision must be able to be seen as a decision in law (i.e. the decision must be able to be seen as being in line with the existing legal material), whilst simultaneously justifying this material and the decision at hand by reconstructing the normative scope and content of it in the best possible way, morally speaking.

[16] See e.g. Dworkin Ronald, *Law's Empire* (Fontana Press, London, 1986), 190ff.

[17] See n. 5 *supra*.

Finnis now claims that there exists a kind of incommensurability between these two dimsensions of legal reasoning (at least when it comes to hard cases). He says[18]:

Even an ideal human judge, with superhuman powers could not sensibly search for a uniquely correct answer to a hard case (as lawyers in sophisticated legal systems use the term 'hard case'). For in such a case, the search for the right answer is practically incoherent and senseless, in much the same way as a search for the English novel which is 'most romantic and shortest' (or 'funniest and best' or 'most English and most profound').

Finnis underscores this point by reference to the notion of intransitivity of value. If we have three possible outcomes A, B and C, it might be the case that according to criterion x, A is valued higher than B and B higher than C, but according to criterion y, C is valued higher than A. If we are to make a decision according to x and y, it is not possible to make a rational choice. This is a piece of logic which is useful as Finnis employs it, as we noted above, against 'emaciated' conceptions of practical reasoning evident in Game Theory and its analogues.[19] But as a critique of Dworkin's theory of legal reasoning (where x and y correspond to 'fit' and 'justification') it is question-begging in that it simply assumes and asserts rather than demonstrates that 'fit' and 'justification' are incommensurable criteria, in the sense that they cannot be weighed against each other. True, as Finnis points out, Dworkin does not proceed very far in presenting an account of how the two dimensions must be weighed and balanced, but this does not entail that it is generally not possible to do so.[20] Of course, there may be doubt about what the right answer is, and therefore it is important, as Finnis notes, to stress that the decision (choice) which is being made by the (majority of) the highest court holds authority for the whole community (legal system). [21] But this is not to say that the decision or choice

[18] Finnis (n. 13 *supra*), 143–4.

[19] See n. 10 *supra*.

[20] Finnis (n. 13 *supra*), 145.

[21] *Ibid.*

cannot be guided by further reason. Indeed, if it cannot be so guided it would not be correct to speak about the choice as a *decision* in a hard case.

This is so first because a case which is characterised as a conflict between two incommensurable values (goods, interests) is better characterised as an *impossible* case, rather than a hard case. If the values in question really are incommensurable, then it is impossible to settle the conflict; and we might revisit this point presently. Hence, and secondly, the choice would not qualify as a decision, in the sense that this term is usually applied in a legal context, for a decision with any pretensions to authoritative status in relation to a correlative obligation to obey (as Finnis argues is the case) must, at least ostensibly, be a reasoned resolution of a social conflict. But if the conflict is indeed between incommensurable values, then the case is injudiciable. If the opposite were the case, and it were possible simply to deduce an answer to the conflict at hand, this would also not qualify as a hard case. At two points Finnis makes an argument of this kind against Dworkin's claim about right answers to hard cases. But this, we think, is to misunderstand Dworkin. Finnis says that Dworkin attempts to show that 'a uniquely correct (the right) answer is available in "most" hard cases',[22] and later adds (without direct reference to Dworkin) that 'morally significant choice would be unnecessary and, with one qualification, impossible if one option could be shown to be the best on a single scale which . . . ranks options in a single transitive order'.[23] We might agree with this view in the sense that *perfect* knowledge of a situation and perfect knowledge of a moral principle which would allow for a transitive ordering of goods would grant us no choice in determining how social conflicts ought to be solved. However, and this we have stressed several times, we are not in a position to attain such knowledge, and our situation, therefore, is not so simple. But the point is that it is our constitution as beings with limited intellectual and physical powers located in disparate and

[22] Finnis (n. 13 *supra*), 143.
[23] *Ibid.*, 146.

shifting contexts of conflicting interest that makes choices difficult—not the alleged incommensurability of values.

Dworkin, in our view, would not find this position difficult to
accept; and thus it is an error to portray his position as one of
trying to show that, in a transcendent sense, uniquely correct
answers are available in hard cases. We think it more reasonable
to receive the idea in the sense that a 'right answer' is not a
uniquely correct one (this would presuppose perfect transcendent knowledge), but rather one which strikes the best balance
between 'fit' and 'justification' *bearing in mind* the imperfect
conditions under which we operate, and acknowledging the artificial character of legal reasoning. This latter, as we have con-
stantly stressed throughout, stems from the transformation of
natural moral reason into institutionalised right according to the
logic of the Autonomy Thesis. In relation to both of these points
we must note that although a thorough institutionalisation of
reason is justified, it cannot lead to a situation where law is
wholly severed from morality, for that (as we explained in
Chapters 2 and 5) would simply undermine the entire *rationale*
of law in the first place. And (as we tried to show in Chapters 3
and 4) neither can a call for a *descriptive* theory of law or an
appeal to political 'democracy' change the fact that law must be
seen as a moral concept. Decisions, which constitute the last link
in a chain of reasoning which started from moral premises,
must be made in a way that permits the original reasons to illuminate all the intermediate steps so that the decision can stand
out as coherently as possible. We might say that the aspiration
of 'fit' is an aspiration to make the decision coherent with the
mediated attempts (*via* legislation, previous decisions etc.) to
install a moral order; whereas the aspiration of 'justification' represents the aspiration to interpret these mediated attempts in
accordance with what moral soundness requires. From this perspective, the dimensions of 'fit' and 'justification', rather than
being two parallel lines, are seen to have a common point of
departure. The reason a case presents itself as a hard case is that
the existing legal material presents itself as less than morally
rational, because previous authorities (legislators, judges etc.)

have acted with less insight or resources (morally or empirically) than are available in the case at hand. It is this, rather than an insoluble conflict of values, that makes the case a hard one.

To be unable to make perfect decisions, and to live with the authority of less than perfect regulation, does not exclude the possibility of aspiring towards making the best decisions possible under imperfect circumstances. In this respect we think Finnis' notion of incommensurability is doubly problematic in relation to an issue which we have already touched upon, namely the problem identified in Chapter 2 as that of moral indeterminacy and the development of systems for stabilising control of practical reasoning. Of the consequence of incommensurability, Finnis says[24]:

> In sum: much academic theory about legal reasoning greatly exaggerates the extent to which reason can settle what is greater and lesser evil. At the same time, such theory minimizes the need for authoritative sources. Such sources, so far as they are clear, and respect the few absolute moral rights and duties, are to be respected as the only reasonable basis for judicial reasoning and decision, in relation to those countless issues which do not directly involve those absolute rights and duties.

Here, then, Finnis is arguing that authority for the most part cannot be controlled, and that therefore it must be respected as reasonable. But this raises precisely the problem we have identified in relation to the Autonomy Thesis, in that it propounds the logic of autonomy whilst simultaneously undermining the very reasons for which the thesis was introduced. Authority, as we have already argued, is necessary and important, but not *in its own right* and, hence, not in a morally uncontrollable form.

Attributes of a Theory of Authority and Interpretation

In examining this lacuna in the concept of legal authority, and in the attempt to sketch the conditions of what we have called

[24] Finnis (n. 13 *supra*), 151.

'transparent' autonomy, we might look to the available resources in the field of existing legal theory. The theory we are looking for must, in the context of the complexity of competing interests, offer the possiblity of the formal and public application of systematic and demonstrable principles or criteria of weighting proceeding from a concept of substantive moral rightness. More specifically, as a natural basis for legality a moral theory must operate with the following attributes:

(1) It must offer a logically compelling, that is, a *necessary* demonstration, of the soundness of foundational principles of categorical prescription. No empirical account can achieve this;

(2) It must encompass a general field of actual or potential conflicts of interests. That is, in addition to seeing moral relationships as relationships between individuals, is also alert to the problematic moral status of individual duty *vis-à-vis* the community and vice versa. This entails a logical account of the issue (as Maus reminds us[25]) of whether moral (natural or 'suprapositive') law is (*assymetrically*) exclusively the prerogative of citizens against the state, or might be used (*symmetrically*) by the state against the citizens.

(3) It must offer scope for distinguishing grounded rights claims from mere assertions of unilateral preferences or wants, and for the purpose of, first, avoiding the logical impasse of of a 'collision of duties'[26] and, secondly, to offer some rational basis for a structured attempt to apply its direct principles in indirect contexts subsequent to the institutionalisation of right. In short, it must present some guidance on the determination of a hierarchy of basic 'goods' or principles which might be weighted in accordance with underlying interests.

[25] See Chap. 4, *supra*, n. 3.
[26] Kant says:

since duty and obligation are concepts that express the objective practical *necessity* of certain actions and two rules opposed to each other cannot be necessary at the same time, if it is a duty to act in accordance with one rule, to act in accordance with the opposite rule is not a duty but even contrary to a duty; so a *collision of duties* and obligations is inconceivable—Kant, Immanuel, *The Metaphysics of Morals* (Mary Gregor (trans.), Cambridge University Press, Cambridge, 1996) [6:224] at p. 16.

(4) Finally, it must acknowledge and offer structured guidance in evaluating, integrating and balancing the *moral weight* of formal procedural requirements that follow from the logic of law's autonomy as against substantive direct moral claims arising in litigation and legal reasoning.[27]

Among the writers who have responded to this task, there is some agreement that the idea of striving towards reproducing in legality the kind of inter-connectedness which characterises the organic nature of socal institutions should be a priority. This has been expressed as a basic requirement of not only stable criteria of weighting—as Nils Jansen has acutely observed[28]—but also of 'integrity' or 'coherence' in legal reasoning. Dworkin and Alexy are perhaps most notable in this regard. But before we examine these arguments, we think it important to articulate a fundamental objection to the value of such analyses in isolation. That is, in the complex contexts of policy formation, legislative regulation and adjudication intrinsic to legal reasoning, ideas of 'order' or 'coherence' or 'weighting' seem to *presuppose* rather than provide a *substitute* for some fundamental conditioning criterion of value. Thus there is a problem of logical priority in such a discourse. We will try to show that attention to synthesising a conception of basic goods giving rise to an understanding of basic rights precedes the admittedly indispendable ideas of 'integrity' or 'coherence' and 'weighting'.

The Implausibility of Incommensurability

We think that the best argument against incommensurability of values is simply its inherent implausibility. First, and very generally, if we reason in a manner which Kant would have termed 'analytic', we might start from the fact of authority and retrace the presuppositions inherent in a sustainable construction of the *concept* of authority. This point of departure entails the awful

[27] See our discussion of Radbruch's views in Chap. 2 *supra*.

[28] Jansen, Nils, 'The Validity of Public Morality' [1998] *Archiv für Recht und Sozialphilosophie.*

truth that, if law (authority) is to facilitate the pursuit of the good, then law must acknowledge and encourage the pursuit of the greater good, and judge accordingly when unavoidable dilemmas of policy formation, decision-making and sacrifice arise in the processes of human interaction. If the law or some form of enforceable authority is seen as a *necessary means* to the pursuit of the good, it becomes practically irrational as an institution if it does not respond to practically reasonable priorities of value where clear priorities exist. An institutional failure to acknowledge the existence of such priorities would result in a practically *un*reasonable form of authoritative 'autonomy' from moral reason. Finnis, of course, would accept this much but argue that clear priorities are the rare exception, and that the infinitely greater part of the law can make no reasoned choice. 'Authority' and the concession to a positivistic notion of technical 'validity' in this Finnisian sense arise, then, from a position which denies any reasoned continuity from clear or basic moral priorities (rights/forbearances), to the vast and perplexing range of issues and choices which must come into its daily remit. The important logical point to be drawn here is that it is in no way self-evident or particularly plausible that we should accept that our moral situation is as here described.

That is, given that the rationale for an autonomous normativity—a fount of authority—rests upon an argument which appeals to this overarching power as a *necessary means* to the pursuit of the good, it seems rather odd that we should simultaneously accept that the overwhelming majority of instances of the use of this power has no rational basis in relation to the small set of principles which, apparently, are our only guarantee of the existence of the natural good in the first place. The simple suggestion, therefore, that there might be, in addition to the demonstrable derivation of basic goods, some guide to the derivation of a hierarchy of goods, appears at least *as* plausible as an assertion to the contrary, and more so when we consider that it would, in the context of an 'analytic' form of reasoning, greatly reinforce the moral-practical foundations of the very concept of authority. This, of course, is not an argument against the

Finnisian (or any other) claim that values are indeed incommensurable, but it most certainly concentrates the mind in relation to the logical details of such a claim—*especially when that very claim lays the foundation upon which rests the separation of law's authority from moral validity.*

Let us, then, look at the actual derivation of basic goods and the ensuing thesis of incommensurability in Finnis. They are, as is well known, an excellent exposition, defence and contemporary application of the philosophy of Aquinas. Epistemologically, however, they invite some scrutiny. We might recall that our first suggestion in respect of the requirements of a foundational theory of transparent autonomy was a logically compelling synthesis of the basic concept of right. We must note that, although Finnis suggests that the basic goods are *presuppositions* of practical reason, this seems to be a latitudinous employment of the term 'presupposition' if it is intended to equate to the status of apodictic or dialectically-necessary conclusions. Apodictic or dialectically-necessary presuppositions cannot rationally be denied—that is, the attempt to deny them engenders explicit contradictions. We must remember that, for example, *universalisable* instrumental-prudential maxims as solid as: *he who wills the end must will the means,* are, philosophically speaking, extremely hard to come by; and are rarely (in fact, in these sceptical times, never) uncontentiously received. Thus the inferential standards for what is proposed merely as an instrumental-prudential presupposition of practical reason are extremely high, let alone what is to be accepted *necessarily* as a *categorical* and universally valid *end* to be pursued. We have discussed this at length elsewhere[29] but, broadly and briefly, Finnis's defence of Aquinas suggests that, just as there are necessary and non-tautological presuppostions of theoretical reason, there are parallel truths to be found underpinning practical reason which furnish us with a knowledge of basic goods. There are seven: 'life', 'knowledge' ('for-its-own-sake'), 'play', 'æsthetic experi-

[29] See n. 9 *supra.*

ence', 'sociability' (friendship), 'integrity' and 'authenticity' in our practical reasonableness, and 'religion'. Finnis says[30]:

> those seven purposes are all of the basic purposes of human action, and that any other purpose which you or I might recognise and pursue will turn out to represent, or be constituted of, some aspect(s) of some or all of them.

This is an extremely plausible observation. But the following—on all three counts—is not[31]:

> First, each is equally self-evidently a form of good. Secondly, none can be analytically reduced to being merely an aspect of any of the others, or to being merely instrumental in the pursuit of any of the others. Thirdly, each one, when we focus on it, can reasonably be regarded as the most important. Hence there is no objective hierarchy amongst them.

The use of the word 'hence' in the final sentence is extremely ambitious. But to compound the thesis of incommensurability, Finnis insists that the basic goods are to underpin a philosophical or ethical *method* which comprises nine principles of practical reasoning which, 'as with each of the basic forms of good, each of these requirements is fundamental, underived, irreducible and hence is capable when focused upon of seeming the most important'.[32] The conclusion here, given the assertions which precede it, is perfectly justified but serves only to underscore our dissatisfaction with the thesis of incommensurability. For among the nine principles of method[33] to be employed in reasoning about values or ethics is the injunction to the effect that there must be 'no arbitrary preference among values'. But

[30] Finnis, John, *Natural Law and Natural Rights* (Clarendon Press, Oxford, 1980), 92.

[31] *Ibid.*

[32] *Ibid.*

[33] They are (*ibid.* 104–7): a coherent plan of life; no arbitrary preference among values; no arbitrary preference among persons; detachment and commitment; the (limited) relevance of consequences; efficiency within reason; respect for every basic value in every act; the requirement of the common good; following one's conscience.

this can only lead us to ask how, given that we are to accept the incommensurability of basic goods *and* of the principles of ethical reasoning about them, we might possibly arrive at a *non-*arbitrary decision concerning preferences of value.

The best way to respond to this and other assertions of the incommensurability of values is *not* to start arguing about which values or goods ought to be, or could be, prioritised non-arbi-traily. This begs the question: it assumes, as an argument against incommensurability, that there are indeed commensurable values. But in the absence of a theory of value which furnishes such a criterion of priority or weight, this is a mere gainsaying of the incommensurabilist position. The logic of this observation, how-ever, works both ways, but it does not leave the contending par-ties in an equal position. For, even in the absence of such a criterion, the simple suggestion that some attributes and capac-ities of human striving might be *necessarily* shown to be more important than others—for example, that access to the where-withal of striving *per se* might be more important than the oppor-tunity to experience the pleasures of play, or that certain forms of purely pragmatic knowledge relating to maintaining subsis-tence requirements might be more important than expansive forms of knowledge-for-its own-sake, is infinitely more plausible both inductively and *a priori* than a suggestion to the contrary. This is not to say that empirical instances of sincere human commitment to every possible configuration of values cannot be adduced. But this is entirely irrelevant: this very condition gives rise to the deliberations at hand. Given this problem, and given the sheer implausibility of incomensurabilism, we ought to reject it—simply because we cannot fail to do better. This means, of course, that we must re-examine the detail of what genuinely constitute the presuppositions of practical reason with the express purpose of fathoming a way of determining, in general, our moral priorities.

In jurisprudential terms, the broad antitheses of positivism and naturalism lead us to a crossroads in legal philosophy. The oppositions which arise here stem from the way in which the relationship between the prudential and the moral is theorised.

Depending on the precise mechanisms of inference employed we are either stopped in our tracks at the limits of the instrumental art of self-interest or led beyond prudence into morality and thence into law. The Finnisian account offers an argument which correctly suggests that we attend to the rich substratum of presuppositions which lie beneath the surface features of our unreflective existence as practical reasoners, yet his contention is that the fleeting vision of the good dissolves into value-incommensurability and, effectively, moral paralysis.

Commensurability and Coherence

The principal constituents required of a theory of reasoned authority (and, hence, validity) are (a) an insight into values within practical reason itself which lies deeper than prudence; (b) at least the possibility that practical reason might turn out to provide a hierarchical structure of values which might guide our attempts to weigh and balance interests in authoritative decision making, and (c) the deductively and practically persistent idea that legality must strive to present itself as a coherent and integral whole. Incommensurability threatens to scupper our attempts to realise the possibility in (b), but, as Raz quite rightly observes, with it too goes the hope of coherence.

Briefly, on this latter point, let us note that no-one perhaps, with the exception of Ronald Dworkin, has done more than Robert Alexy in showing us the pervasive value of coherence in the analysis of all aspects of authority.[34] He explains that coherence becomes a requirement for law because the law necessarily raises a claim to correctness, which, in turn, implies a claim to justifiability. Justification comes about through argumentation, and a theory of argumentation in law must look to *consistency*, *comprehensiveness* and *connection*. But, just as incommensurability undermines our attempts to develop a rationally defensible basis for decison-making in the weighing of values, Raz claims that the 'authority-based character of law' is incompatible with

[34] See Alexy, Robert, *A Theory of Legal Argumentation* (Adler, Ruth, and MacCormick, Neil (trans.), Clarendon Press, Oxford, 1989).

a coherence-oriented account in that there exist 'pervasive incommensurabilities among values'.[35] This, of course, resonates with Finnis' claim that too big a role is attributed to reason in the determination of valid law. Coherence of justification in law requires a coherent account of how values—formal and substantive—are adjudged to relate to each other. Coherence, therefore, is not an issue which can be divorced from the problem of weighing; it presupposes the availability of suitable criteria. Let us, then, try to move towards some more optimistic account of the general and compound problem.

Finnis and Raz hold that values are commensurable in so far as they have some common feature according to which the preferability of other competing values can be (objectively) measured. Thus, weighing and balancing commensurable values is a question of giving expression to a pre-existing hierarchy among the values. On this view, decision-making is of a rather passive nature, in that it is values themselves that contain the answer to the problem. In fact, on this view commensurability does not involve any constructive weighing and balancing at all. Conversely, if Finnis and Raz are right, then incommensurability makes weighing and balancing impossible, and this in turn paves the way for a disembodied and novel notion of 'authority' to plug the gap where practical reason runs out. But there is one very obvious drawback here in relation to problems which, for lawyers, increasingly arise: *that a lack of reason for a decision cannot be invoked as a justification for the use of authority.* Judges, fortunately, are forced to be more creative than simply referring to the authority of their position. If no criteria for weighing and balancing exist, and no rational attempt at a narrative of coherence can be presented, then lawyers have to develop them. If this means that we must say that incommensurable values become *artificially* related to each other by *actively creating and fixing* certain preference relations between them, so be it.[36] But we must note that this way of solving problems of value-

---

[35] See Raz, Joseph, 'The Relevance of Coherence' *Boston University Law Review* (1992) 72, 309, at n. 64.

[36] See Alexy (1998) (n. 34 *supra*), 47.

pluralism in legal conflicts, though it is brought about by *adding* evaluative criteria, does not make the weighing and balancing arbitrary or irrational, neither does it remove law in its entirety from morality. Rather the opposite is the case, in that the introduction of what Nils Jansen calls 'weight assignment criteria', enhances the capacity for reasoned choice. Jansen explains[37]:

> In public discourse weight assignment criteria determine the weights of freestandingly justified principles. They express what is important for public morality and therefore what 'counts' in freestanding discourse. They thereby assess the *validity* of moral norms. He/she who sets such evaluation criteria, determines which is the stronger or the weaker argument and thus makes normative statements with implications that are not neutral.

Jansen is aware of the acute possibiliy of value conflict at the level of moral and political discourse in complex pluralist societies and says[38]:

> As weight assignment criteria are categorically different, they may run counter to each other. They therefore require *a principled structure* which enables varying weight assignment criteria to be taken into account *simultaneously* [our emphasis].

Determinate Presuppostions of Agency

Those who have been at once most supportive of the project we undertake in this book have fortunately been the most critical.[39] It has not escaped their notice that we have elsewhere and over a period of time subscribed to the value of an argument which purports to show that prudential reason implies a deep structure

[37] Jansen (n. 28 *supra*), 12. Jansen offers a fourfold criterion of weight assignment, the first part of which is a cognitive principle: 'The weights of a principle of public morality increase as the degree of intersubjectivity of its justification increase': (*ibid.*), 13. We ask the reader to consider this in the light of our remarks concerning the theory of determinate presuppositions of agency *infra*.

[38] *Ibid.*, 13.

[39] The King's College London seminar series 1999—*Constructing Constitutions*—has been a valuable forum. We are grateful to all participants for their comments on these and related matters.

of morality, the principles of which are *dialectically necessary* in the sense that all agents, on pain of contradiction, must support these principles.[40] This argument, developed by Alan Gewirth, analyses the nature and implications of the determinate presuppostions of agency in the attempt to ground a universally valid basis for moral claims. It is important to stress that we do not regard this argument as a *deus ex machina* which might conveniently resolve all our problems. We suffer from no such illusion, but introduce this argument primarily because of the urgency and centrality with which we regard the purely formal problem of the inferential move (within the analysis of practical reason) from the *prudential* to the *moral*, and its bearing on what has emerged as the definitive problem of the characterisation of 'artifical' reasoning in law: that of the *indirect* application of norms. Thus with the advent of what we have earlier referred to as an ecumenical trend towards the general acceptance of the necessary connection between law and morality—what William Lucy has called the *entente cordiale* between positivisms and naturalisms—we see that what can easily degenerate into ambiguity and vacillation is actually a reluctant acknowledgment of the futility of sustaining false and entirely uninformative oppositions. The impasse in the analysis of legal validity and obligation must, in our view, initially relocate itself in terms of moral phi-

[40] See Toddington, Stuart, *Rationality, Social Action and Moral Judgment* (Edinburgh University Press, Edinburgh, 1993); Olsen, Henrik Palmer, *Rationalitet, Ret og Moral* (DJØF, Copenhagen, 1997). See also, more recently, our joint works 'Legal Idealism and the Autonomy of Law' in *Ratio Juris* 12:3, 1999 and 'Idealism for Pragmatists' *Archiv für Rechts- und Sozialphilosophie* 4/99. The argument in question was first introduced by Alan Gewirth in his *Reason and Morality* (University of Chicago Press, Chicago, Ill., 1978). Our interest lies with the formal structure of the argument, which we believe forms a better starting point than the Habermasian strategy, which relies on problematic notions of intersubjectivity and of the epistemic value of consensus. See Habermas, Jürgen, *The Theory of Communicative Action* (Heinemann, London, 1984) and *Between Facts and Norms* (Polity Press, Cambridge, 1996). We also believe that Gewirth's analysis of the dipositional features of agency forms a suitable starting point for an analysis which, in the Dworkinian sense, is to strive for the highest possible level of integrity: see Dworkin, Ronald, *Law's Empire* (Fontana Press, London, 1986).

losophy, and here the Gewirthian argument offers a valuable opportunity for a genuinely epistemological point of departure in contemporary jursiprudence. This argument has a formal structure which coheres with the four theoretical criteria listed above.[41] It presents us with a purely logical (i.e. non-moral) step of universalisation of prudential reasoning which *necessarily* implies determinate moral commitments and, further, offers a basis for the orderly and systematic weighting of basic goods in the indirect application of the fundamental principle of morality in complex contexts.

The analysis of the origin of rights is presented in terms of a series of what Gewirth refers to as *dialectically necessary* claims from within the standpoint of the idealised agent. Simply, the contention is that an act of voluntary agency presupposes the valuing of an *end* or goal, and thus the valuing of the *means* to achieve it. Generically, the wherewithal to act for *any* end or purpose is to be seen as a *necessary means* and must be valued as such. On this basis a prospective purposive agent must, dialectically speaking, consider it impermissible for any other agent to interfere with this generic capacity. To fail to take this position is contradictory from within the standpoint of the prospective agent. This amounts to the dialectical requirement to claim *rights* to one's generic well-being. The crucial and, many have suggested,[42] contentious step from this prudential position is made as follows[43]:

---

[41] See the subheading 'Attributes of a Theory of Authority and Interpretation' *supra* p. 144, *supra*. We repeat that it is important at this point that any alternative arguments, e.g. the Habermasian argument for communicative foundations of morality, be judged against these 4 theoretical criteria in respect of its ability to form a viable basis for structuring and weighing various rights claims. As an introduction to such a consideration, the reader may refer to White, Stephen K., 'On the Normative Structure of Action: Gewirth and Habermas' (1982) 44 *Review of Politics* 282ff. and Toddington (n. 40 *supra*), chaps. 7, 8.

[42] See the discussion in Toddington *ibid.*, 179–83.

[43] See Beyleveld, Deryck, *The Dialectical Necessity of Morality* (University of Chicago Press, Chicago, Ill., 1991), chap. 3, 52–3; see Alan Gewirth's account in 'The Justification of Morality' (1988) 53 *Philosophical Studies* 245–62 at 245. On the absolutely crucial point of 'universalisation'.

Since the necessary and sufficient reason for which the agent claims these rights is that he is a prospective agent, he must accept . . . 'I have rights to freedom and well-being because I am a prospective agent.' Hence, by universalisation, he must also accept.' All other prospective agents have right to freedom and well-being.' Now this is a moral judgment, because it requires the agent to take favorable account of the interests of all other prospective agents.

From here (and this is the substance of our argument in regard to commensurability and weighting), the central contention is that right-claims must be prioritised relative to their necessity for the 'generic' and, importantly, *'dispositional'* features of action. 'Action' is here to be understood as the voluntary and purposive shaping of one's behaviour. The generic and dispositional features of action consist of those elements that, further, accommodate and support a person's capacity for voluntary and purposive activity. These elements can be characterised as 'freedom and well-being' in so far as freedom and well-being is understood as the term which denotes the general set of physical, cerebral and emotional attributes and resources necessary as means to all and any pursuit of a person's freely chosen purposes. Where Finnis suggested, perhaps rightly, that the values which conditioned our purposive strivings might always be seen as compounds of all, or some, of his (or Aquinas's) conception of the basic goods, the notion of the generic and dispositional goods of agency are undoubtedly more fundamental. They are not rightly seen as goods which lie among our basic values, but rather as goods which underpin all our possible aspirations as *general means* to any hope of *successfully* realising them. There is, of course, a fluid transition from the most indispensable and efficient to the dispensable and inefficient of these means. In thinking about these means it is important to be aware that the focus lies with the *generic-dispositional* features of action. Deryck Beyleveld says[44]:

My basic well-being, like my freedom (both dispositional and occurent), is a generic feature of my agency in an all-inclusive sense,

[44] Beyleveld (n. 43 *supra*) 19–20.

being necessary for my pursuit as well as my achievement of my purposes. Non-subtractive and additive well-being may also be given generic-dispositional interpretations, not as particular purposes and the contingently necessary conditions for their specific achievement, but as abilities and conditions to retain and expand one's capacities for particular actions in general. As such they are generic features of my agency in the all-inclusive sense. They are not necessary conditions for my pursuit *per se* of my purposes, only necessary conditions for generally succeeding in achieving my purposes.

The point of introducing these levels of generic features of action is to make possible a weighting of right-claims. Such a scheme of weighting is, as we have argued, a *sine qua non* of the quest for a form of legal authority which might be regarded as *transparently* autonomous from natural morality. Such a weighting is made possible by the fact that the various elements in the theory of the determinate presuppositions of agency can be seen as being more or less indispensable or efficient in relation to a person's general ability to pursue and succeed in achieving his or her freely chosen purposes. In other words, the various elements of the generic features of action fall into a hierarchy determined by the degree of their indispensability for purposive action in general. Using this hierarchy to prioritise among right-claims, we can derive the general principle that the more the fulfillment of a right-claim is indispensable or efficient for the general ability to pursue one's freely chosen purposes the higher priority it should be given. Having said this, we should, of course, remain aware that the determination of these judgements of priority will appear as a contentious matter in the face of competing claims from different perspectives of interest. However, we must, even at this very general stage, at least acknowledge that we now have some insight into *which interests* should be prioritised and a frame of reference for discussion of *how* they ought to be evaluated in relation to each other.

This, of course, is merely a thumbnail sketch of a theory which can but point in the general direction of how a commensurabilist strategy might develop. But it does illustrate the kind of moral epistemology which must be developed if we are serious about grounding our public and practical deliberations aimed at achieving real resolutions to conflicts of interest. Only on such a commensurabilist foundation, we maintain, does it make sense to speak of the 'weighing of interests' or the quest for 'coherence' in the law.

Validity and Obligation

We see no sensible point in prolonging the traditional debate concerning the 'necessary' or 'contingent' relationship between law and morality. The crucial interdependence of law and morality, both conceptually and practically, is not seriously open to question. The issue is whether or not, and in what form, morality can survive the transformation from its natural state, through the process of institutionalisation and autonomy, to the situated and shifting contexts of its indirect application. Whatever this form might take, it is always characterised by an interplay between legal form and moral interpretation. This relationship must be made explicit in the legal decision, and the very notions of authority and legitimacy demand that we are able to retrace and reveal the normative background for the decision. If we place this in the light of our discussions of the implications and presuppositons of Postema's account of the Autonomy Thesis, we can formulate this as a demand that the need to establish *some* form of normative autonomy for legal authority should make the *transparency* of this autonomy an essential condition of its legitmacy. Such transparency is a condition of the validity of the system and, hence, of the particular decisions taken within the system. Legal validity and the correlate condition of obligation coincide when the legacy of natural and pre-legal morality is made to shine through the formality of autonomous law.

Index

159

Index